More Praise for *The She Spot*

"The principles of **Marketing to Women** are as true for social change as they are for products and brands. I applaud the Lisas—Witter and Chen—for applying them to such a good cause. Women are always striving to improve the world, and their book lays out the case convincingly."

> — Marti Barletta, Founder, the TrendSight Group, and
> author of **Marketing to Women** and **PrimeTime Women**

"Finally, the book I've been waiting for that connects the dots between the research on what women want and actionable ways to reach them. I recommend it to any nonprofit or political candidate who wants to tap into the women's vote and their power as donors and activists."

> — Celinda Lake, President, Lake Research Partners, and
> coauthor of **What Women Really Want: How American
> Women Are Quietly Erasing Political, Racial, Class, and
> Religious Lines to Change the Way We Live**

"If you're in the business of social change, you need the information in **The She Spot**. Transforming the world can only happen if you understand what this book has to say about what women value, how they operate, and how important they are to making change happen."

> — Barbara A. Brenner, Executive Director, Breast Cancer Action

"**The She Spot** proves that women are at the forefront of power and change and shows executives of all types how to reach them. Finally, concrete steps to better tapping women's potential."

> — Ilana Goldman, President, Women's Campaign Forum

"I am buying a copy for everyone I have ever worked with! The authors prove that marketing to women is so much more than turning everything pink, and most importantly, **The She Spot** tells you how."

> — Morra Aarons-Mele, blogger and Political Director,
> BlogHer.com

"Want to connect with the rising tide of world-changing women? Ditch the pink logos, petunias, and pandering. Let this book show you how to supercharge your campaign, company, or community with powerful stories, open and insightful conversation, and opportunities for action that actually fit the way smart women live in the 21st century."

— Alex Steffen, Executive Editor, WorldChanging.com

"This book taps into a truth that labor organizers learn in the shops: women don't just hope and wait for change, they fight for it. When motivated and mobilized, women do change the world, and this book gives us the tools to make it happen."

— Amanda Cooper, Director of Communications,
UNITE HERE!

"'Add women, change everything.' That's The White House Project's prescription for transformation. The change we seek so passionately can only be delivered by adding our nation's most untapped natural resource. *The She Spot* is 'spot on' about how we get there."

— Marie Wilson, President, The White House Project,
and author of *Closing the Leadership Gap: Add Women,*
Change Everything

"By claiming 'they are the audience,' *The She Spot* is the book that gives women the opportunity to claim their space as key agents of social change. In return, this is a must read for those who want to change the world and believe that the road to success is making sure women are at the table and active."

— Christine Grumm, President and CEO,
Women's Funding Network

"This book is a brilliant no-brainer that unlocks a treasure chest of fascinating insights. It's sure to generate an 'aha' moment for save-the-worlders everywhere."

— Ricken Patel, Executive Director, Avaaz.org

THE **SHE SPOT**

THE **SHE SPOT**

Why Women are the Market for
Changing the World
— and How to Reach Them

Lisa Witter and Lisa Chen

Foreword by Gary Hirshberg, CEO Stonyfield Farm

BK

Berrett–Koehler Publishers, Inc.
San Francisco
a BK Business book

Berrett-Koehler Publishers, Inc.
235 Montgomery Street, Suite 650
San Francisco, CA 94104-2916
Tel: (415) 288-0260   Fax: (415) 362-2512   www.bkconnection.com

Ordering Information

Quantity sales. Special discounts are available on quantity purchases by corporations, associations, and others. For details, contact the "Special Sales Department" at the Berrett-Koehler address above.

Individual sales. Berrett-Koehler publications are available through most bookstores. They can also be ordered directly from Berrett-Koehler: Tel: (800) 929-2929; Fax: (802) 864-7626; www.bkconnection.com

Orders for college textbook/course adoption use. Please contact Berrett-Koehler: Tel: (800) 929-2929; Fax: (802) 864-7626.

Orders by U.S. trade bookstores and wholesalers. Please contact Ingram Publisher Services, Tel: (800) 509-4887; Fax: (800) 838-1149; E-mail: customer.service@ ingrampublisherservices.com; or visit www.ingrampublisherservices.com/Ordering for details about electronic ordering.

Library of Congress Cataloging-in-Publication Data
Chen, Lisa, 1973-
    The she spot : why women are the market for changing the world and how to reach them / by Lisa Chen, Lisa Witter.
       p.   cm.
    Includes bibliographical references.
    ISBN 978-1-57675-472-6 (hardcover : alk. paper)
    1. Women consumers—United States.   2. Social marketing—United States.
    3. Women in nonprofit organizations—United States.   I. Witter, Lisa.   II. Title.
HF5415.332.W66C44 2008
658.8'34082—dc22   2008009811

First Edition

12   11   10   09   08   10   9   8   7   6   5   4   3   2   1

Text design by Detta Penna

Copyedited by Kathleen Rake

For my parents, for teaching love by living love.
Lisa W.

For my mother, for all she has taught me.
Lisa C.

Contents

Foreword

I have coached competitive soccer for 12 years. My first eight years were primarily spent with boys ranging from 9 to 19 years old as my two sons, now 19 and 17, progressed from the hornet-swarm stage where the entire team followed the ball, until they exceeded my ability to teach them anything new. For the last half-dozen years, I've mostly led my daughter's teams of girls aged 11–16. The only things that have united these two experiences are the uniforms, turf, balls, and nets. Every other aspect has been so completely different that I'm convinced I've actually coached two different species.

Coaching boys was pretty cut and dried. It was essentially a matter of channeling their testosterone so that the 11 individuals on the field actually managed to move the ball in one direction and toward the goal. They each got the "goal" part from a very young age. They were mostly all capable of putting their heads down and plowing up the field, until they pounded the poor ball or some opposing kid. The challenge was to get them to remember that they were not alone on the field and that they needed to operate in tandem with their mates. In other words, the dilemma was how to mold them into a team. My pre-game and half-time speeches about how to cooperate and work together have always yielded mostly monosyllabic and undecipherable grunts. Even today, as I watch my son and many of my former players on their college varsity teams, I still have no clue what is going on between their ears.

The experience with the girls could not have been more different.

The day I took over as coach of my daughter's team, I was stunned by how naturally and harmonically the girls instantly formed into a squad. The "I's" disappeared seamlessly into a "we" as they selflessly passed the ball in a cooperative dance. And when I spoke, they listened, asked questions and—imagine this—even responded. There was never any guessing about where their heads were at for they were VERY open to discussing the "process." However, getting them to focus on the game, and the "goal," has been entirely another challenge.

Soccer is a team game, and these girls have all of the skills and instincts to function as a group. But that harmony can disappear in one snap of the finger depending on who said or did what to whom. With the boys, there is only one feeling brought on to the field and that is an utter hatred of their opponent. Their basic instinct is to kill, topple, and maim from starting to ending whistle.

But the girls refuse to leave their feelings on the sidelines. They bring a whole new, complex, and unpredictable set of emotions into the game with them. They can hate or love their opponents, their teammates, the refs, coaches, parents, or the dogs barking in the neighborhood. If they are losing or tied, or if they don't like their opponents' looks or behaviors, they can be twice as vicious as the guys, but if they are winning by too much, the empathy kicks in and they will often help a knocked-over opponent get back up. The team's emotional tenor can swing violently over the course of a match.

Unlike the boys, the girls' worst injuries have been of the emotional sort. When one boy's ankle gets banged up, we lose him, but when one of the girls gets her spirit wounded, I can lose the entire team in a swift empathetic cyclone that strikes within seconds.

There's another big difference between my soccer boys and girls. Ask the boys the score and they can tell you in seconds. Ask the girls the score and you get 11 different answers. But ask which teammate went to the dance last night, who is sitting with whom in the stands, how many opponents have braces on their teeth, or what their coach is wearing, and they can tell you these things in exquisite detail. They are serial connectors—to each other and everything that is around them.

My wife is the same way. I can be at a gathering for four hours and have no clue about the personal histories of anyone in the room, whereas Meg can tell me the life stories of most people there within 30 minutes of arriving.

It is with these constantly recurring observations and experiences that I can vouch for the inherent power of women to emote and empathize, to connect to one another and operate on an intuitive level that is entirely foreign to guys. And as a founder/CE-Yo of a national brand that depends completely on building an emotional bond with my mostly female consumers, I am deeply convinced that this insight can lead to a powerful mobilization of economic and political power. But this is not a power to be taken for granted, for the sword can swing both ways. Building a bond of loyalty with women requires an absolute and unwavering fealty to the virtues that the brand or product stands for. Breach that contract once by compromising or wavering from a religious observance of those virtues, and like my soccer girls, the harmony can disappear in a heart beat.

Stonyfield Farm is celebrating 25 years in business. We have grown an average of three to four times faster than has the entire U.S. yogurt category over the last 18 years. We are now the largest organic yogurt brand in the world and the third largest U.S. yogurt brand. As I've reflected on the reasons for our success, I have developed a thesis that I have captured in my new book *Stirring It Up: How to Make Money and Save the World*.

Lisa Witter and Lisa Chen present an argument that is entirely in harmony with my brand-building experience. Stonyfield has achieved these remarkable growth rates with a marketing budget that is practically a rounding error in comparison to those of our leading competitors. To be clear, our successes have nothing to do with any type of advertising or traditional consumer "acquisition" strategy. Ours is not an intellectual relationship with our consumers based on "features and benefits." We have instead created what I call a "handshake" with our mostly women consumers—a bond of trust, comfort, and loyalty that is immensely powerful. Ours is a word-of-mouth brand, built on the strength of satisfied consumers telling others about "their" yogurt brand.

We have "connected" with our audience of connectors, and the benefits have been entirely mutual. We have fed them and they have fed us, and among the results is that the money we would have spent on advertising has instead been invested in our yogurts, to achieve better taste and health. We also use profits to convert farms to organic methods that are not harmful to the earth, and, through our profits-for-the-planet program, we make substantial donations to countless charities. All these investments have created a bond of loyalty with our alert, empathetic customers who of course want to feel better about not only what they put into their and their families' bodies, but about the brands and companies they support as well.

This really is not rocket science. After all, loyalty is the holy grail of consumer products, brands, or political candidates. The least expensive way to obtain your next purchase or vote is to get a current customer to buy again. And when a consumer is loyal, and feels rewarded, she tells her network. Not only is that endorsement far more powerful than any media spend or bundle of gross rating points, but it can become contagious with a life of its own, spreading from community to community, much like the many examples of viral marketing you'll read about in these pages.

It's not science, but it is art. Building and maintaining loyalty requires that you never breach the bond of trust you've established with your connected consumers. It is about being honest. It is about never promising more than you can deliver, and always delivering on your promises. And it is about heart. The mostly female audience we serve needs to know that we are genuinely trying to make the world a better place. As long as we keep investing in activities that protect and restore their health and the health of the planet, they will remain on our side. But the minute we violate that trust or are not accountable and forthcoming about any breach, we can lose them forever.

As women become more and more aware that we truly are what we eat and feed to our families, they are seeking alternatives to sugar and corn syrup solids. And so, for example, the purveyors of sodas are beginning to find themselves in an evolutionary dead end. And if you think I'm crazy, just look at the spate of acquisitions or divestments by the soda and other big food giants in recent years, and the extraordinary prices they've paid for alternatives like Sobe, Vitamin Water, Odwalla, Naked Juice, or Honest Tea. Indeed every large food company in America has bought or invested in an emerging organic brand. It's because they see the market "organically" drifting towards not only natural and healthy offerings, but away from the poisons that make us obese, cause diabetes, cancers, and more.

It's too bad that many of these giants have not in fact decided to concentrate on making the world a better place, because in the long run that would be better for them, and for all of us. Better for them, because that's what women, in increasing numbers, want. Like my soccer girls, women are tuned in and connected to the world around them. They may not have the time or interest to picket or protest, but they want to feel good about the brands they support. And better for us, because business truly has the power to expedite the changes we need to make the planet healthier and safer.

At Stonyfield, we feed those good feelings by all that we do. We are 100% organic. We buy milk and all ingredients from family farmers and we pay them a fair and sustainable price for their quality goods. We use only organic ingredients—no artificial sweeteners, dyes, or thickeners—and we refuse to compromise even when it would make us more profitable. We give 10% of our profits to environmental efforts. We use our packaging to promote causes that help foster a healthy planet. We were the first manufacturer in America to offset 100% of the CO_2 emissions from our manufacturing, a full decade before the release of Al Gore's film. We built a waste treatment facility that generates its own clean-burning gas that we use to run the facility. We collect used yogurt cups and turn them into toothbrushes and flower pots. We formed a new nonprofit called Climate Counts to stimulate climate activism, which you can read about later in this book.

I am convinced that these are the reasons we are growing so fast.

The really cool thing about this argument and this book is that Lisa and Lisa are showing us a way that we just might be able to save the planet. By marshalling the forces of loyalty, connectedness, empathy, and the desire to make our purchase dollars count for something good, we just might be able to persuade business to increase investments in cleaning up the mess we've created for future generations. To me, that is the most important message of this book, as well as my own. As my late friend Anita Roddick used to say: "Anyone who thinks they are too small to make a difference has never been in bed with a mosquito."

Women *are* connectors. And most women get the fact that we aren't exactly leaving our children and grandchildren such a great deal. They are beginning to get the idea that they can use their purchase power to redirect resources and activities towards preventing pollution, climate change, and war. Like with my soccer girls, the key is to stimulate the natural tendency of women to feel, to seek solutions, and to coalesce as a team to march in lockstep toward these essential goals.

Lisa and Lisa have pulled together some brilliant insights and examples. I have no doubt that their unassailable arguments about how to successfully leverage the transformative power of women in today's society will excite many men and women to explore the bountiful opportunities of cooperation—with both nature and ourselves. I am honored and humbled to introduce this superb and inspiring book, and am grateful to the authors for their hopeful contribution.

Gary Hirshberg
Londonderry, NH

Preface

What Is the *She Spot?*

A few years ago during the 2004 election, a coalition of get-out-the-vote organizations asked Lisa Witter to advise them on their "Women's Voting Day" campaign, including the beta design for the campaign's Web site.

When she clicked on the URL, the home page was wreathed in pink flowers. The content was focused exclusively on choice and "soft" issues like education and healthcare to the exclusion of issues like the War in Iraq, jobs, and national security—issues that polling showed were, in fact, top-of-mind for the majority of women voters.

The coalition deserved credit for identifying women as an important target audience. But then they hit two blind spots that, as communications consultants for the public sector, we see all too often: One, by relegating their outreach to women to a single "day," they were missing out on an enormous opportunity to connect with the demographic powerhouse that has shaped presidential elections for the past 20 years. Two, their efforts to appeal to women were off the mark, reflecting a poor understanding of what women actually care about and respond to.

We wrote this book to correct these blind spots and find the She Spot instead. By "She Spot," we mean taking to heart this central truth: **Women are not a niche audience. They are *the* audience.** Losing these blind spots and finding the She Spot starts with recognizing that women are the single most important market opportunity for changing the world. This is something that many nonprofit organizations know intuitively, but have yet to fully explore or harness.

By taking a closer look at women as the target market for change, you may discover some new insights. Among them:

- As philanthropists and donors, women take more risks than men. They're more likely to give to a new or less well-known organization they believe is truly making a difference than, say, their alma mater, a museum, or other well-established institution.

- Women are more distrustful of the political process than are men. This is reflected in their giving: they're more likely to donate to nonprofit organizations than to political candidates.

- Women do not use a gender lens when choosing their favorite candidate. They won't favor a female candidate over a male one just because she's a woman.

- When it comes to women's voting preferences, marital status trumps many other factors, including age, education level, and motherhood. In other words, a single woman in her 30s is more likely to vote in sync with an older widow than a married thirty-something mom.

- More women than men are online today, and more women are blogging.

- African American women give more than white women, but get actively solicited for donations less often.

Our own work with women's foundations and donor-advised funds suggests that women are especially invested in addressing the root causes of social ills, such as poverty, childhood obesity, or pollution in our drinking water. This willingness to confront and insist on change at the *structural* level, versus applying short-term Band-Aids to temper the symptoms, should make every nonprofit that lives by the same creed prick up its ears.

We hope the gender differences discussed in this book will provide you with a deeper understanding of the mindset of women so you become savvier "She Spotters" and more effective at cultivating women's support to scale the greater good you want to see in the world.

In our work as communications consultants, our initial conversation with new and prospective nonprofit clients invariably comes down to two key questions: *What is your goal?* and *Who is your target audience?*

The goal varies depending on the organization. It can involve preventing a dangerous gas plant from being built near a wetlands sanctuary or raising funds for disaster relief. But there is often one unwavering constant: fundraising and action are critical for success. *Great*, we say. *What does your average donor look like? Who makes up your membership base?*

Whether the organization is an environmental group, a social welfare fund, or a progressive political organization, the answer is *women*.

The She Spot grew out of a combination of our frustration, our hope, and our belief that women are an untapped, unsung yet essential force for transformative social change in our world—a force that is needed today more than ever before.

Frustration, because too many who work in the public sector are not connecting the dots between the change they want to see in the world and the people most likely to realize that change. We want to help make that connection.

Hope, because in the field of international development, it is now a widely accepted fact that investing in women is the single most effective strategy for rebuilding nations torn apart by war and other violent conflicts. In Rwanda, the 1994 genocide that claimed more than 800,000 lives, most of them men and boys, left the nation with a population that was 70 percent female. It was up to the women to rebuild the economy, the government, and the future of the country. Women became breadwinners, taking on jobs traditionally held by men.

Before the genocide, the government was just over five percent female. Today, the Rwandan Lower House of Parliament is nearly half women, the highest percentage of women in any parliament in the world. Girls and young women are attending school and college in record numbers. Many of them are the same women who were gang-raped, who saw their families butchered before their eyes, and who lost entire social networks to mass slaughter. Yet they are rebuilding their communities, taking in one orphan at a time, weaving one basket at a time, passing one piece of legislation at a time. Their resilience and fortitude in the face of unfathomable tragedy has produced an incredible come-back story of national transformation.

It takes nothing away from these remarkable women in Rwanda to say that this is something women, who are the glue that holds communities together, have done throughout history, and continue to do today in many nations struggling to come back from war. Professionals who work in international development often say that the key to lifting communities is to invest in women. This is not rhetoric for the sake of annual fundraising appeals. It is an on-the-ground reality and pragmatic policy. In our own country, it is women who are often holding families together in communities ruptured by the War on Drugs, or holding down the fort and taking care of business as their husbands fight wars overseas. There is no "over there" versus "back here" split when it comes to jumpstarting social transformation. Women are at the center. The difference lies in how women catalyze, or fail to catalyze, their power.

This book is also a product of our belief—belief that the public sector could borrow a few pages from the business sector's playbook when it comes to marketing to women. Innovators in the corporate world understand that women are behind more than 80 percent of all consumer purchases and all health care-related decisions for their families, which is why many companies have begun to retool their marketing campaigns to appeal to this critical audience with a level of sophistication that goes well beyond painting their products pink.

These are lessons the nonprofits and political operatives ignore at their own peril. As we'll reveal in these pages, women's contributions to philanthropy, to determining elections, and to volunteering make them an essential "get" for those of us committed to making the world a better place.

That said, you don't have to be a nonprofit professional or a staffer on a political campaign to gain something from reading this book. The ideas and tactics we explore are also meant for individuals who are interested in how social and political change is achieved and what it will take to tackle some of the biggest challenges facing us today, from global warming to stopping nuclear proliferation. This book is also meant for individuals who are engaged in making change at the community level, either by serving on community boards, at church, or with the local PTA. In each of these instances, we'll show how hitting the She Spot can move the needle and make a difference.

What You'll Find in These Pages

This book is divided into three parts. In Part I, we make the case for *why* centering your marketing efforts around the *She Spot*—women—is an essential strategy for advancing your cause. In Part II, we show you *how* to effectively connect to women so they become your partners in social change, and in Part III, we look at *where* to reach them.

The Introduction explains how the business world has caught on that women are the most important consumer market and what the public sector has to gain from following the same path. In Chapter 1, we discuss why going after the women's market is essential for any social change effort by describing how women can tip the balance for fundraising, activism, changing social behaviors, and winning elections.

Chapter 2 digs deeper into the neurological and psychological research that helps to explain the similarities and differences between how women and men think. We then describe how these differences shape what matters to them in life and their decision-making and how you can use this knowledge to help cultivate women's support for your issues and causes.

What matters to women is the subject of Chapter 3, which takes a look at polling data and other sources that tell us what women's social priorities are and how these priorities are shaped by their roles at home and at work.

In Part II, we put theory into action by showing you how the ideas outlined in Part I can be practically applied based on four core principles: *care, connect, cultivate,* and *control.* We show you that by keeping these principles top of mind, you will hit the *She Spot* and market to women more effectively.

Chapter 4 discusses women's profound capacity for empathy and how to harness it as a force for change. We offer concrete ideas for how to speak to her heart through dramatic storytelling, humor, and appealing to her sense of group identity.

Women place a high value on relationships. Chapter 5 describes how to actively create community as a catalyst for activism and fundraising. We show how "high touch" campaigns can help recruit women—and men—for your cause and why this approach will yield greater, long-term returns than traditional membership appeals.

Fundraising professionals will tell you that women often require more time and effort to win over. Chapter 6 explains women are worth it because once they're on board, they are loyal and incredible word-of-mouth foot soldiers. This chapter offers strategies for cultivating women's participation and leadership by speaking directly to their concerns and expectations. We argue that meeting the "higher bar" that women set for everything from consumer products to causes increasingly reflects the same expectations that funders and donors are setting for potential grantees.

Chapter 7 is about control and how putting a woman in the driver's seat will make her your powerful ally for doing good. We describe a woman's day-to-day reality and how her concerns and priorities shape her bottom line. We offer concrete marketing strategies that will help leverage her "can do" confidence and make activism and giving a natural extension of her busy life, instead of something that falls off her long to-do list.

In Part III, we offer a road map for finding the *She Spot* by reaching women where they are. In Chapter 8, we examine the media sources women rely on for information as well as their behaviors and preferences as consumers of mainstream media and as members of the rapidly evolving online community.

While the central argument of the book requires that we make some pointed generalizations about women and what makes them tick, we acknowledge that no two women are alike. In Chapter 9, we turn a microlens at the women's demographic by segmenting them along important life stages and identifying how milestones in a woman's life can open new opportunities for marketing change. We also examine the growing influence of the emerging majority—African American and Asian American women and Latinas—and offer advice on how to achieve effective, culturally fluent outreach, while avoiding the pitfalls.

Each chapter illustrates key marketing principles, with real-life case studies drawn from both the business and nonprofit sectors to give you concrete ideas that will translate to the world of good causes. In addition, each chapter explains which adjustments you must make to account for the important differences between the two worlds.

In the concluding chapter, we take a speculative look into the future by posing the question: *What if women's "we're all in this together" way of thinking became the driving force behind social transformation?* If we were to replace the dominant social paradigm of "Survival of the Fittest" with another, "Survival of the Connected," what impact would it have in our social evolution, and how would it affect our ability to take on the biggest challenges facing us today, from global warming to terrorism? We make the argument that marketing and privileging the values most commonly associated with women—cooperation and community among them—has the power to change the way we govern and to transform the very fiber and function of our role as protectors of our planet's future.

While we touch on research and the latest brain science that illuminate the differences between men and women, this book is not meant to be a thorough scientific analysis of these gender differences. Similarly, while a portion of the book provides analyses of a few key sub-groups within the female demographic, we acknowledge that our analysis is not exhaustive. For example, we do not segment our analysis along other lines, such as geographic differences, diverse faiths, or sexual orientation. While these segments are important, we have chosen to drill down on key audiences (women of color, single women, and mothers among them) that we believe are the most likely to be useful for the largest swath of nonprofit organizations and political campaigns seeking to absorb and apply to their own work the strategies and tactics described here. In defining these parameters, we fully acknowledge that each of the topics and audiences described above is fully deserving of exploration, but they are, unfortunately, beyond the scope of this book.

Finally, while this book is aimed primarily at helping social change workers market more effectively to women, we hope to illuminate two things in the process: One, when we don't examine how marketing, advertising, and other communications campaigns work or don't work along gender lines, this lack of scrutiny can perpetuate business-as-usual assumptions that tend to privilege male preferences and perspectives. Two, marketing to women results in an inclusive, rather than exclusive, strategy for reaching men, too, thanks to ways that women typically make decisions to support and otherwise take action on behalf of the causes they care about.

Why Listen to Us?

Our views and expertise in marketing social causes is shaped by a combined 25 years' experience in the field of nonprofit communications, including more than 20 years as senior strategists at Fenton Communications. In the 1980s, David Fenton started the company to go head-to-head with public relations campaigns waged by corporate flacks, front groups, and right-wing spin-meisters, who were molding public opinion on everything from nuclear energy in our neighborhoods to environmental toxins in our food.

A lot has changed in two decades. We've been fortunate to be in either the driver's or passenger's seat as social change advocates used communications to secure legislative, legal, and court-of-public-opinion victories.

One of the things we love about our jobs as consultants is that we're allowed to immerse ourselves in the work of so many different nonprofits, influencing an amazing range of issues that we care about. The constant change-up that comes with the territory gives us a broad and eclectic outlook.

Lisa Witter is the daughter of a union mill worker and a Vietnam veteran diesel mechanic manager, who taught her the ethics of hard work and the value of family, social justice, and community service—values that were reinforced at the church she went to while growing up in Everett, Washington. As a youth, she was active in soccer, volleyball, basketball, and softball—it was on the field and court where she first learned teamwork, strategy, and how to play to win. Since then, she has married her passion for people and competitive spirit with the art of politics, working in the political sector to fight for systemic progressive social change.

Lisa W.'s career encompasses a variety of experiences, from her stint as campaign manager for the first Latina to run for statewide office in her home state of Washington, running a successful national campaign to stop the privatization of Social Security, and as one of 10 candidates on the Showtime reality show, *American Candidate*, to her role as a political and social commentator and speaker at conferences and universities across the country. She is passionate about communications and believes that the social change sector must hone its communications skills to effectively realize concrete victories for people. As chief operating officer of Fenton Communications, she has led and grown the largest public interest communications firm in the country, consulting on a broad range of domestic and international issues including women's and refugee rights, environmental protection, public health, socially responsible business, working family and union issues, civic participation, and more.

Lisa Chen's perspectives and grounding in social change work have been heavily shaped by her family's experience as immigrants from Taiwan. Her mother, who left high school to raise two daughters, went back to school at the University of California, Berkeley and became a software engineer. Her stepfather, the son of a factory worker in a small town outside Birmingham, Alabama, joined the army during the Vietnam War, where he learned Chinese and developed a passion for Chinese furniture making. Her parents' earlier struggles—and their will to reinvent themselves—fuel her optimism and her drive to do social justice work.

Lisa C.'s love for language and belief in the power of words as tools of truth and persuasion can be attributed in part to having to learn English at the age of five. She worked for many years in public interest communications as a publicist for Communications Works, a San Francisco-based nonprofit public relations organization, where she managed a number of campaigns on immigration and welfare policy reform, environmental justice, affirmative action, breast cancer, and affordable housing. As a senior vice president at Fenton, she is the firm's senior writer and editor, developing campaign messages and strategy on a broad range of issues including international public health, human rights, education, environmental protection, and the arts. Before getting into progressive communications, Lisa C. was a reporter for the *San Jose Mercury News*.

In writing this book, it was our intention to act as both guides and translators between the private and public sectors, offering our perspectives, insights, and analysis on how social change agents can use marketing to promote and advance social causes and to inspire others to do good. It is our hope that by putting women more firmly at the center of communications efforts, we will help nonprofit organizations and political campaigns exponentially raise their effectiveness in creating a better world.

This book represents much more than an accumulation of our own ideas and experiences. We are in debt to the many smart communicators and marketing experts who were generous enough to share their wisdom with us.

Many books have been written about how to harness the potential of women consumers as an *economic* opportunity. This is the first book devoted to springing open the potential and power of women as our greatest opportunity for social change. Social and political trends of the past 15 years have created palpable momentum behind the idea that women's time is *now*. She's setting the pace. It's up to us to keep up—and spot her.

20% of the profits from this book
go to two of our favorite nonprofit organizations,
Women for Women International
and
MomsRising.org.

Introduction

A Women-Centered (Marketing) Revolution

The Home Depot of today is a lot different than it was ten years ago. The stores feel less cluttered and more airy. Everything, from light fixtures to carpet samples, is more stylish and varied. Home décor departments have been expanded. The company's ad campaigns and catalogues, which used to simply showcase products, now feature more people. In its first six months, a new store feature, "Do-It-Herself" workshops, drew 40,000 women.

Stonyfield Farm grew from being a seven-cow organic farming school in the early 80s into a company with $250 million in annual sales. Every cup of Stonyfield yogurt bears a personal message from the CEO and founder Gary Hirshberg. Turn the lid over and you'll find tips on how to make the world a better place. Stonyfield was ahead of the curve when it came to products that had special appeal to moms, like Yo-Baby yogurt and calcium-fortified yogurt. All of this has been critical to the company's surge as the fastest-growing yogurt company in the world.

The success of these companies are representative of a sea change in the business world in the past 10 years as business leaders have come to recognize women as much more than an "emerging" or niche market. Today, women represent the largest and most important consumer market there is.

How did this happen? It began with demographic changes among women themselves in their roles at work and at home. Today, women make 83 percent of all consumer purchases—everything from breakfast cereal to big-ticket items like cars and personal computers—for themselves and for their families. They are also responsible for 80 percent of all health care-related decisions for their households.

Wising up to the power of the purse and its ripple effects in the marketplace, smart companies began putting female customers first by thinking creatively and critically about what they want. They shaped the consumer experience to appeal to women from the minute they walk into the store or click on the company Web site, all the way through the point of purchase.

As marketing gurus Tom Peters and Marti Barletta put it, there is "a widespread recognition among business leaders of the blazingly obvious . . . that women are where the money is."

Yet the nonprofit and political sectors have been slower to pick up on this demographic revolution. Not only do women have the power to profoundly influence the world of consumer goods, they also have the power to rouse and accelerate our ability to *do* good—provided we know how to unleash that power.

Why Women Are the Key to Moving the Needle on Social Issues

But wait, the skeptic in you is asking, *What does selling kitchen tiles and yogurt have to do with securing universal health care or curbing global warming?*

The answer is *a lot*. Because women as a group affect much more than the consumer marketplace. Research shows they are also the pistons that keep the engine of most nonprofits running successfully and are key in determining the outcome of political elections and campaigns. Consider the following:

- **Women give**. Conventional wisdom suggests that because men as a group earn more money, it follows that they give more to charity. Wrong. Women actually give just as much, but they give differently. Women control over half of the total wealth in America, and all evidence points to their inheriting and managing more wealth in the near future. Women also account for roughly 60 percent of socially conscious investors. The 2008 election has also proven to be a milestone year in women's political giving, with women making donations to candidates in unprecedented numbers.

- **Women volunteer.** Women, particularly mothers and women who work, volunteer at significantly higher rates than men, according to a 2006 federal study. Across the nation, about 32 percent of women volunteer compared with 25 percent of men. These findings have financial consequences as well: studies show that volunteers often make gifts on average two and a half times more than non-volunteers.

- **Women vote.** Since the 1960s, women have turned out in higher numbers at the voting booth. Women made the difference in the 2006 mid-term elections, accounting for the decisive margin in a number of close races that ultimately shifted the balance of power in Congress.

- **Women pay it forward.** Women are inherently community-minded and love to seek advice and share good information when they have it. This makes them ideal "connectors" and foot-soldiers for advocacy or fundraising campaigns. What's more, and as described in more detail later, what "works" for women often clicks with men as well.

- **Women are behind major social movements.** Throughout American history, women have been a major force behind important social movements, from the abolition of slavery and the temperance movement, to the suffragist and civil rights movements. Their roles may not have been written in the history books, but these social reforms could not have occurred without their leadership and support.

Doing a better job of marketing to women does not mean that we neglect or forget men in the process. As we'll discuss in greater detail later, the experience of corporate marketing campaigns has shown that when you market to women's concerns and meet their higher expectations on return, you will sweep up men's support as well. In other words, hit the She Spot and you'll hit the He Spot, too.

Why Gender-Neutral Marketing is Not Enough

Many of us are comfortable with and, indeed, support the idea that campaigns targeting youth or people of color be tuned into nuances, into differences between these populations and the perceptions held by them if they are to succeed. Yet when we talked to people about the concept behind this book—why it's important to market differently to women than to men—we encountered enthusiasm from some ("It's about time!") and resistance from others who expressed concern that calling out gender differences threatens to undermine the hard-won notion that women and men are equal and should be treated equally.

It's worth noting that these different reactions were more or less split along generational lines, with Generation X and Y women in the positive camp, and some baby boomer women taking a skeptical, even wary position. It's not difficult to see why: women who came of age in the 1960s have had to fight precedent-setting battles for equality with men; women of younger generations hold social and political perceptions shaped as inheritors of their legacy, including the cultural shifts that grew out of the second-wave feminist movement.

When it comes to improving the lives of women and girls and creating the society we want to live in, we couldn't agree more that women should be treated on equal footing as men. But we are selling ourselves short if we deny the fact that gender differences exist. These differences are supported by a body of scientific evidence that shows that differences in male and female brain structure, chemistry, and hormones shape our different priorities, preferences, and approach to the choices we make in life. We see these differences in action by watching how little boys and girls behave on the playground. And they affect us as adults as we make decisions about everything from what we buy, to who we vote for, to which causes we choose to champion.

Culture, of course, has an enormous influence as well. At work, at home and at play, and in their relationships with others, men and women take on different roles that shape their priorities, attitudes, and preferences. If we ignore the real differences between how men and women think and perceive the world, we significantly cripple our own efforts to appeal and activate the audiences we need on our side.

In short, women *are* from Venus and men *are* from Mars. But for too long, traditional marketing and outreach approaches have placed men's worldviews and preferences front and center, marooning women on Mars and crippling their ability to recognize women as a critical audience requiring sophisticated communications strategies if we are to reach them.

It's About Her

Those of us in the public sector got into this line of work because we care passionately about righting wrongs, protecting the environment, and helping people. But it's a mistake to think that simply getting the word out about "the issues" will convert people into taking up worthy causes.

In the early days of marketing and advertising, it was enough for a business to sing the praises of a product's attributes, whether shampoo or headache medicine. But in today's competitive marketplace, where store shelves carry five or more brands of essentially the same product, a straight description of attributes is no longer a persuasive selling strategy. That's why modern-day marketing campaigns focus much less on the product, and much more on the *prospect*—the needs of the customer.

Marketing in the nonprofit sector must make a similar conversion. Today there are 1.4 million nonprofits in the U.S. competing for a limited pool of dollars. Public sector organizations must combat "compassion fatigue" and a thickening fog of information overload. Meanwhile, political candidates and statewide ballot initiative campaigns are challenged to drum up support and voters, many of whom are cynical and disengaged from the political process.

In light of these challenges, it's more important than ever that public sector professionals rigorously re-examine *how* they're communicating to their target audiences—and *who* that target audience is. It's our argument, of course, that the audience is women, and that the first step in marketing to them effectively is to rid ourselves of the notion that women are a niche audience. In other words, ditch the niche. The steps after that make up the meat of this book, where we describe the elements involved in creating marketing efforts that appeal to the things women care about and respond to.

We're sympathetic to nonprofit staff for whom the idea of reformulating their organization's marketing and outreach efforts to be female-friendly can sound overwhelming. But don't panic. Keep these things in mind:

- Marketing to women is not about adding another layer to your communications as you would add an extension on your house.

Remember, women are not a niche. They are *the* audience. Once you take this to heart, you'll see that what you're doing is pouring cement in your communications foundation, building in this approach rather than adding on. As we'll get into later in the book, women have built-in attributes of their own that make them a sure return on your marketing investment.

- You won't have to start from scratch. Chances are you're already applying a few (or more than a few) of the marketing tactics that women respond to. Our hope is that, in the future, you'll do so more intentionally, and become even more sophisticated and effective in your application.

- The bottom line is this: Just as the rules of the game have changed in the consumer marketplace, they've changed in the social change marketplace as well. Busy lives, shortening attention spans, data overload, competing demands—these are factors that define modern life and have conspired to make it tougher to break through. To do more than survive and actually thrive in this environment, the public sector must do a better job of marketing by looking through a prospect-focused rather than a product- or issue-focused lens. Because when we successfully connect with our target audiences in deep and personal ways, we build loyal and longer-lasting relationships with donors and members that strengthen our organizations and bolster our ability to make change on the scale necessary to truly make a difference in people's lives.

The Four Cs: Care, Connect, Cultivate, and Control

Based on our own field experience as communications consultants for nonprofit clients and our research into corporate marketing practices, we've identified four key principles to effectively marketing to women. They are:

- **Care.** Most people choose to do good not because they've reasoned it's the logical thing to do, but because their sense of caring and empathy has been triggered and it becomes the right thing to do. When we strike directly at the "heart" of our issues, we unleash an emotional response, the necessary first step to engagement.

- **Connect.** Women place a premium value on creating community in their lives. They understand that the ties between people are the force that make the world go round—and forward. When we tap into this powerful force, we honor people's deep-felt desire to connect with others, and help build a movement for progressive change.

- **Cultivate.** Women are tough customers who take decision-making seriously. If they've signed up to support your organization, it's because you've successfully addressed their check-list of concerns. Once they're on board, however, they more than pay it back by being true believers and loyal supporters who turn around and cultivate new donors and members on your behalf.

- **Control.** Remember our prospect versus product argument? This marketing principle is about working within, not against, women's busy, multi-tasking lifestyles and leveraging their hopeful, take-control approach to life to creating a better future for all of us.

These marketing principles are especially effective at reaching women, but, as we'll show, they work for men as well—and this is no accident. Our goal is to help sharpen your marketing senses and help you cast aside misguided assumptions regarding gendered marketing that may be inadvertently tuning out or turning off women and preventing you from identifying opportunities that can help you actively appeal to them.

The smarter and more effective we are at reaching women, the better our chances of deepening their commitment, of moving them from the transactional (cutting one check or signing up for a one-time volunteer gig) to a deeper sense of responsibility that inspires more meaningful and, ultimately, more seismic change at the social and cultural level.

Marketing—for Social Change

Some of us may be unaccustomed to the idea of "marketing" as an approach for reaching target audiences to achieve social change goals. Still others may be skeptical about using lessons borrowed from the business sector, considering that corporations have been responsible for many social ills that nonprofit groups are working to fix, from environmental pollution to economic disenfranchisement. Beyond these concerns, there may be others still who are wary that marketing directly to women adds another troubling dimension—that of manipulating this critical demographic to serve specific interests.

But remember, marketing strategies and tactics don't hurt people; people hurt people. If you're reading this book, chances are you aren't in the business of selling tobacco or expanding your oil drilling ventures. You're in the social change business, and your goals make all the difference. So does the level of respect, sensitivity, and insight you bring to your marketing efforts as you seek to reach women and bring them on board.

Indeed, as Katya Andersen points out in her book, *Robin Hood Marketing: Stealing Corporate Savvy to Sell Just Causes*, "There is no nobility in preaching to an audience of one." As change agents, we have an ethical responsibility to ourselves, to our work, and to the people who support us—financially and as activists—to fully harness tools that time and experience have shown make us more effective as communicators and bring us closer to transforming the world for the better.

We must also remind ourselves that social change sector audiences are often the same people who corporations target to buy cars or switch to their brand of fabric softener. They are the same people who are receiving direct mail appeals from groups working in opposition to your goals. And these same people must filter an unprecedented *tsunami* of information—from billboards and magazines to the Internet and TV advertisements—from the minute they wake up to when their heads hit the pillow.

The organizations and companies that break through the data smog are the ones that use smart, sophisticated strategies that appeal—and connect—directly with their target audiences. This is the power of effective marketing.

We must also remember that if we do not take a more sophisticated approach to marketing, with an eye for how particular messages or tactics may or may not appeal to women, we may, at best, be unintentionally sidelining this important audience, and, at worst, unintentionally applying a male-centric approach to our outreach. This would not only do women a disservice, it undermines our best efforts to create a groundswell of support for the causes we believe in.

In the next chapter, we take a closer look at why women are the key market for the public and political sectors by examining the power they wield in pulling the levers of change: service, giving, voting, and taking action.

Part I

Understanding the She Spot

1

Why
Women
Matter

Women: A Nonprofit's Best Friend

A few years ago our colleagues at Fenton were working to rebrand Infact, a venerable nonprofit organization that burst on the scene more
than three decades ago with a successful worldwide boycott of Nestlé.
The food giant was aggressively marketing its brand of baby formula to
mothers in developing countries. The only problem was, the formula
for making the formula—add water and stir—was hurting and, in some
cases, killing infants because some local water supplies were too polluted
for their young stomachs.

The organization had since developed a formidable track record
of forcing major corporations, including Big Tobacco, to the table to reform their abusive business practices. As part of the rebranding process,
we asked them who their target audience was. They replied, "women."
Specifically women in their 40s to 60s, because they made up the group's
core funding base and were also their most loyal and active members.

This isn't true for all nonprofits, of course, but it is for a surprising number of them, including ones that work on issues that are not
considered traditional "women's issues." The progressive online group,
MoveOn.org, for example, has more than three million members; the
average donor profile is a woman in her mid-40s. Women give, and what
they give can help make the backbone of an organization.

So as Infact was rethinking their name (they are known today as

Corporate Accountability International), our colleagues made sure their new and improved identity system spoke to their base. Part of this involved shaping their message and their mission—fighting bad-guy corporations—so neither strayed too far from the "why" driving their work. Their organization tagline today is, "Challenging Abuse. Protecting People."

Transforming Society As We Know It

Women's growing economic and political clout in the private and public sectors can be traced at its origin to the 1940s when, for the first time, women left the home for the workplace in unprecedented numbers in response to the labor shortage created when many men went off to war. In many ways, women have never looked back.

Following this group of pioneering women were the baby boomers, many of whom would become radicalized during the 1960s and give rise to the feminist movement. For the first time in our history, instead of following traditional female roles, a significant number of women were calling their own shots when it came to making money, taking a political stand, and deciding for themselves what they wanted out of life.

Times, they're still changing. In 2007 the latest census figures showed that, for the first time in history, single women outnumber married ones in the U.S.

This shift has been shaped by a confluence of social factors: more women are postponing marriage while others are living unmarried with partners. Women are also outliving their husbands and, compared to divorced men, divorced women are delaying another trip down the aisle. William H. Frey, a demographer with the Brookings Institute, described the shift to the *New York Times* as "clearly a tipping point, reflecting the culmination of post-1960 trends associated with greater independence and more flexible lifestyles for women."

Taken as a whole, all these trends have produced seismic changes in the home as well as in the labor force. They are transforming philanthropy and the nonprofit sector as well. Today, women are arguably the most important audience (and a driving force) for those of us who do social change work. Here are six reasons why:

1. Women's economic clout is growing.

On one level, it boils down to money: who's got it and who's giving it. Given that women continue to earn 78 cents for every man's dollar, you'd be inclined to think men control the majority of the wealth in this country.

But a recent survey of data from the Federal Reserve Board reveals that this isn't so. Women actually control slightly more than half (51.3 percent) of all personal wealth in the United States. They make 83 percent of all household purchasing decisions, including big ticket items that are typically associated with men: cars, home development wares, and home electronics. Women even buy more riding lawn mowers than men do.

There are several reasons for this slight income edge. One is that women outlive men, and widows are inheriting their husbands' wealth. But that's just one sliver of the pie. Women are also generating their own income as never before, to the point that one out of four married women out-earn their spouses.

Women-owned businesses today are the fastest-growing sector of the U.S. economy, representing $3.3 trillion in purchasing power. What's more, firms owned by women of color are growing at six times the rate of all U.S. firms.

This is just the tip of the iceberg. There are strong indications that women will continue to level the playing field with men as their income as a group continues to rise.

One of these indicators is education. Today, more women than ever are getting a college education, the biggest stepping stone to higher-paying jobs. What's more, once women start attending college, they are significantly more likely than men to graduate (63 percent compared to 55 percent), according to recent studies.

On average, women are still earning less than men. But when they complete their college degrees, they're making greater leaps than men in raising their standard of living. This trend makes college education a profound predictor for women's greater income potential in the near future. Between 1990 and 2000, the standard-of-living gain for women with a bachelor's degree under their belt compared to those with a high school diploma was 13 percent larger than for men.

We're already seeing these trends play out. The number of women who earn $100,000 or more has tripled in the past decade, making them the fastest-growing segment of wealthy individuals, according to the Employment Policy Foundation. Over the past 30 years, women's income has jumped more than 60 percent, while men's median income has stayed (more or less) the same (up just 6 percent). This phenomenon shows no sign of letting up. Women from the baby boom generation are at their earning peak. And as Americans live longer and healthier lives than their parents, many are planning to forego the retirement community in Florida in favor of working well into their so-called "golden years." By 2010 women are expected to control 60 percent of the country's wealth, which makes them a prime target for fundraising by nonprofit organizations and political campaigns.

2. Women care—and give.

But how much you make isn't necessarily a reflection of how much, or whether, you give to good causes.

For decades, the traditional face of philanthropy has been the Fords and Rockefellers of the world, titans of industry who established large foundations in their names to organize their giving. Bill Gates and Warren Buffet are modern-day exemplars of that model.

Yet by focusing our attention too narrowly on the giant checks, we risk losing sight of how philanthropy is changing, and how women are driving this change. Women make contributions to twice as many charitable organizations as men do, and they are more likely to take greater risks in organizations with a strong vision for change. There are also strong indications that women are closing the giving gap, driven in part by the earning trends alluded to earlier and the greater control they are exerting over their personal wealth.

Also, many women who have it, give it—and they give it big. A survey of nearly 400 prominent American businesswomen found that more than half donate $25,000 or more a year to charity; 19 percent give $100,000 or more a year. Even more striking, high–net worth women business owners with assets of more than $1 million are even more likely than their male counterparts to contribute at least $10,000 a year to charity (50 percent for women compared to 40 percent for men).

On the political front, women are giving in unprecedented numbers to presidential candidates in the 2008 election. As we write this, women account for more than half the contributions to Hillary Clinton's and Barack Obama's campaigns. The boom in female political donors has been attributed to mounting frustration with the situation in Iraq, support for Hillary as the first female candidate with a real shot at the White House, and to a general push by women for a sea change in political leadership and the direction of the country.

While these trends are promising, they are just a hint of what's to come. It is a core contention of this book that women's financial might has yet to be tapped to its fullest potential, and a lot of that has to do with how good a job we're doing at marketing to them. If we were to apply marketing strategies that truly spoke to women's hearts as well as their bottom lines, they would respond in even greater numbers.

What motivates women to give is the subject of a later chapter, but it is worth noting up front that women's giving is not necessarily limited to issues traditionally associated with women and children, although education does tend to top the list of priorities. It's also important to know that, while men tend to donate out of organizational loyalty or to support the status quo (like their alma maters), women are more committed to giving money to organizations and causes they believe will bring about social change.

Women are putting their money where their mouths are in more ways than giving. Their commitment is also reflected in their numbers in traditionally caring professions, from nursing, teaching, and social work to the public sector, where women head more than half the foundations in the country and 70 percent of program officer positions.

3. Women pay it forward.

Money, of course, is not the only important force for change. Many nonprofits rely on a strong membership base to achieve their advocacy goals. This is one area where women can, and have been, phenomenally influential.

Lisa C.'s friend Kim recently bought a pair of Dansko clogs when she saw a colleague at Smith College, where they both teach, wearing a pair. "Those are cute," she said. "Are they comfortable?" The friend enthusiastically sang her shoes' praises: "I wear them all the time!" On that strong endorsement, Kim bought a pair for herself, but experienced a fleeting pang of buyer's remorse when they hurt the first time she wore them. But within a few days, the clogs were comfortably broken in. When Kim's fiancé's sister saw her wearing her Danskos, she asked about them. Kim gave the clogs her own positive review, along with the tip that they take a few days to wear in. Now the sister owns a pair, too.

Kim did what many women do every day—pass good information forward. In other words, when you market well to women, you also benefit from the world's most powerful marketing tool: word of mouth. Word of mouth is more prevalent among women than men. Not only are women less shy about asking outright for tips on what to buy and how to save, but they're also more likely to volunteer such information. Clairol capitalized on this power to great effect in a memorable advertising campaign that showed a woman telling two friends about the remarkable shampoo, and her friends each telling two friends, "and so on, and so on."

For nonprofits seeking to build their visibility or political candidates seeking to gain support, women who are true believers can help make believers of others by spreading the good word to friends and family or by simply giving their honest appraisal of why they're voting for a candidate or supporting an issue.

Women's word of mouth can be credited for wildly successful fundraising campaigns like "Race for a Cure," the Susan B. Komen Foundation's annual fundraising marathon for breast cancer. As well, nonprofit groups like MoveOn.org are increasingly using social networking tactics such as word of mouth to build communities of activists—a topic we'll explore in greater depth later in this book.

4. Women can tip the election.

Maybe it's because women didn't get the right to vote until the passage of the 19th Amendment in 1920, but more women than men have voted in every election since Lyndon B. Johnson was in the White House.

In the 2006 midterm election that ushered in the first Democratic Congress in 12 years, 51 percent of the electorate was women compared to 49 percent men. According to a nationwide survey by *Ms. Magazine* and the Women Donors Network, 55 percent of women voted for Democratic candidates compared to 50 percent of men. This five-point gender gap was enough to make the difference in a number of close races. The African American women's vote was credited for being the determining factor in Democratic Senator Jim Webb's victory in Virginia.

The gender gap was also alive and well in the 2004 presidential election, with women seven points less likely than men to vote for George W. Bush. Back in 2000, the split was even more pronounced, with women 10 percentage points less likely than men to vote for Bush. In both elections, the majority of women favored the Democratic candidate.

If the pollsters and pundits are to be believed, the outcome of the upcoming 2008 presidential election may well be determined by the single woman. Single women—a group 47 million strong that includes the Carrie "Sex in the City" Bradshaws of the world as well as widows, twenty-something college grads, and divorced single moms—has been something of a sleeping giant in politics, mostly because neither the Republican nor Democratic Parties have really invested the time to listen or speak to their concerns. The candidate who builds the bridge stands to reap enormous gains on election day.

5. Women volunteer more of their time.

About 65.4 million or 28.8 percent of American adults volunteered in 2004–2005, according to a recent study by the Bureau of Labor Statistics. This represented a 30-year high in volunteering. And women are leading the way. About 32.4 percent of women volunteer compared to 25 percent of men, and more women than men are volunteering across every state and across all age groups, education levels, and other demographic measures. When you average all the data, it's possible to paint a profile of the typical American volunteer: a female who gives 50 hours of her time per year.

What's more, women with children under the age of 18 and women who work have higher volunteer rates than other women. The fact that working mothers, the very individuals you'd think would have the least amount of "free" time, are holding up the high end of the service spectrum may strike some as counterintuitive. It's not. As we'll explore in later chapters, for many women, being a mom and being part of the workforce means deeper connections in the community, and a deeper commitment to making things better for the future as well as the here and now. Volunteering is one way to act on those connections and commitments.

The fact that mothers volunteer in significant numbers has a ripple effect because young people from families where their parents and/or siblings volunteered are more likely to volunteer themselves. This is great news for the estimated three in four charities that use volunteers, the majority of which say volunteers are critical for the success of their overall operation.

After all, time is money, and the value of volunteer time adds up. Using Independent Sector's estimate of the dollar value of a volunteer's time ($18.77 per hour), the value of the three billion hours of volunteer service in 2005–2006 add up to an estimated $56.3 billion. Women can claim responsibility for providing the bulk of that pot.

6. When you "sell" to women, you reach men, too.

When Sheryl Hilliard Tucker, the executive editor of Time Inc., was an editor with *Money* magazine, *Money* conducted focus groups of men, who represented the majority of their readership, to get a better sense of what they wanted out of the magazine. Tucker and her colleagues discovered that they didn't necessarily just want to be smarter about the issues, but they want to know how to make smart choices. In other words, men said they wanted the same thing from their business magazine that has been a defining feature of women's magazines for decades: practical, real-life advice. Today, the banner headlines on men's and women's magazines are remarkably similar. *Cosmopolitan* promises to give you the low-down on how to get a flat stomach in 10 days, while *Men's Health* claims to have the secret to achieving killer abs in, yes, 10 days.

"Women like service, whether they feel confident or not confident. *Men's Health* has been successful by basing itself on a women's magazine formula, but for men's topics. Men don't like to admit they like service, but they do," according to Lynn Povich, co-chair of the International Women's Media Foundation and a former senior editor with *Newsweek*.

Women's hunger for, and openness to information is what makes them, in many ways, tougher customers than men. They demand more information before they make decisions, whether it's buying a stereo system or donating to a nonprofit. For this reason, many corporations have figured out that when they meet women's higher expectations, they also increase customer satisfaction among men. In *Marketing to Women*, Marti Barletta describes how the Wyndham Hotel chain took their female customers' suggestion to install magnifying mirrors in the bathroom so they wouldn't have to lean over the sink to apply their make-up. Turns out men use them, too—for shaving.

In the case of charitable contributions, more women than men tend to want to know how exactly their money will be spent. By being more transparent in connecting the dots between donations and the services your organization provides, you'd be providing value to men and women alike.

Will appealing to women ensure that you'll appeal to men, too? Not always. Men and women have their differences, as we'll explore in the next chapter. But the general principle still stands: when you appeal to the toughest customer, you'll have covered the bases on many of the factors that can turn a "maybe" into a "yes"—whether your target audience is a man or woman.

Women are at the forefront of all the primary drivers of change: money, volunteer service, and the power of the vote. This is why they are *the* primary target audience for nonprofits and political campaigns. A closer examination of their standing in these arenas helps crack open some chestnuts of conventional, but misguided, wisdom. Among them: that women's income (and giving potential) lags behind men; and, by appealing to women, you'll drive men away. In fact, just the opposite is true in both cases.

Conclusion

So if women hold the keys to the king- or queen-dom, what does it take to unlock their potential? "Potential" is the operative word here because, while we've demonstrated why women matter, making them count is a whole other story and the driving force behind this book. Because women have been perceived as a niche audience for so long from both the public and political sectors, we are light years behind where we should be in marketing to them to unleash their power as partners in social change. But before we dive into tactics, we'll spend the next two chapters getting a better grasp on how women think and what they want, both of which are essential primers for the marketing principles that follow.

Chapter Take-Aways

Women are the primary target audience for nonprofits and political campaigns because:

- Their earning potential and economic clout is growing.

- They give—to more than twice as many charitable organizations as men do.

- They're great at spreading news by word of mouth, which makes them natural marketers.

- Their vote tips elections. More women than men have voted in elections since 1920.

- They volunteer more than men; moms with kids at home have even higher volunteer rates.

When we take a closer look at these drivers, we crack open some chestnuts of conventional, but misguided, wisdom such as:

- Women's income (and giving potential) lag behind men's. In fact, women control slightly more than half of all personal wealth in the U.S.

- By appealing to women, you'll drive men away; just the opposite is true.

2

How
Women
Think

Gender Differences vs. Gender Equality

This book is premised on the fact that men and women are fundamentally different, which means they view things and respond to them differently, approach problems differently, and make decisions differently. If there were no gender differences, there would be no need to write this book.

By acknowledging these differences, our intent is not to prove that women are better than men, or vice versa, but to point out that often what passes for "gender neutral" marketing is, however unintentional, code for marketing with a male audience in mind. And when men's historically privileged perspectives and experiences come to stand in for all of human experience, it's women whose voices and experiences are sidelined. This is how women came to be perceived as a niche market in the first place, and why we've been subjected to countless consumer products wrapped in pink. Instead, by articulating gender differences, we hope to put women in their true place—away from the sidelines and fully into the mainstream where they belong.

That said, we recognize that underlining these differences can be difficult for some, especially those who have been raised to believe in equal rights for women and rally against gender discrimination in all its forms. The motto for these struggles has been, "women are no different from men, so they should be treated no different from men."

But we want to make an important distinction here: "difference" is not the same as "equality." You can believe in gender differences yet full-heartedly support equality between men and women. Denying these differences actually creates a false reality that does more harm than good.

By way of analogy, consider Ward Connerly's crusade against race-based policies. Connerly, a former University of California Regent, successfully banned affirmative action at California's public colleges and universities on the platform that we are a "colorblind society."

The next statewide initiative he engineered, however, failed at the polls. Connerly's goal was to forbid public institutions, including public health departments and law enforcement, from collecting data based on race. But this time Californian voters rightfully balked because the majority understood that color-blindness, while a utopian ideal to some, is far from a present-day reality. The same can be said of the will to cast our society as gender-neutral by insisting that men and women are alike when, in fact, everything from our biology to the way men and women are socialized flies in the face of it.

Yes, Virginia, There is a Difference

A friend of ours, Liz, recently organized an 11th birthday party for her son and 10 of his friends. She described a harried day that included treating the boys to a movie, where they received free promotional posters, which they promptly rolled up and used to beat each other. At home, it was all she could do to keep them from hanging off the light fixtures. As the mother of two boys, Liz wasn't surprised, but she still couldn't stop herself from sighing at their, well, boyish behavior.

Girls wreak their own kind of havoc (think slumber party), but it would be hard to imagine a group of them beating each other en masse or engaging in impromptu wrestling matches on the living room floor. When girls get together, they are much more likely to engage in "pretend" play where made-up interpersonal relationships are part of the fun. From an early age, we recognize seemingly innate differences between the two genders.

These common, everyday observations ("boys will be boys") have a scientific basis. Thanks to relatively recent technological and medical advances, we now have a broader window into how the brain works and how hormonal differences affect behavior. We've come a long way from the days of phrenology, a crack science invented by German physician

Franz Joseph Gall that claimed to identify innate moral and intellectual faculties from reading the tell-tale bumps on a person's skull.

Calling out gender differences is fraught with landmines, of course, as former Harvard President Lawrence Summers learned the hard way when he suggested that women didn't have the intellectual aptitude to succeed in science and math. Throughout history, dubious scientific theories have been used by everyone from criminologists to Nazis to "prove" racial and gender inferiority. Bad science even drove one American psychologist to conclude that the cause of childhood autism was frigid mothering.

Little wonder, then, that many of us are highly suspect when scientific experts draw a link between biological determinism and social behaviors and development. But the solution is not to close our minds to what science has to teach us. As social scientist Carol Tavris put it, "Information itself is neither sexist nor racist; it is neutral." It is up to us to approach scientific findings with a healthy and vigilant skepticism of those who would exploit and abuse science to validate their social agendas. And it is up to us to recognize that, ultimately, human beings are creatures of both biology and social conditioning. The better understanding we have of these influential forces, the more in tune we'll be with where our audiences are coming from so we can tap into their willingness to take action for social good.

Size Doesn't Matter, but Structure and Chemistry Do

Our understanding of how the brain works has grown by leaps and bounds over the past 20 years. Behavioral biology, a relatively new field of study that includes gene mapping and brain imaging, is rapidly transforming our understanding of our differences—including the differences between men and women.

We know, for example, that men's brains are, on average, three ounces, or 15 percent, larger than women's brains. But bigger doesn't mean better, or smarter. What does appear to account for real gender differences are brain structure and brain chemistry. Men and women's brains are literally wired differently.

In her book, *The Female Brain*, Louann Brizendine, a neuro-psychiatrist at the University of California, San Francisco, describes how, viewed under a microscope, the differences between male and female brains are complex and widespread. These differences in the structure, function, and chemistry of our brains affect our perceptions, behaviors, and priorities. Male and female brains have different floor plans, and we use different "rooms" in our brain to solve problems and process language and experience.

Women: The Great Communicators, or the Science on *Connect*

Take the *corpus callosum*. This cluster of tissues and fibers connects the two hemispheres of the brain and enables the flow of information between them. In women, the *corpus callosum* is thicker and more bulbous than in men, which means more information flows between the right and left sides of their brains. Research shows that when this is the case, communications skills and fluency are stronger, which explains why women generally score better on verbal tests and why connecting with other people makes them tick. It also offers a scientific explanation of the phenomenon known as "female intuition." It turns out this seemingly uncanny ability can be attributed to the female brain's ability to "read" even the most subtle social cues, from vocal tones and body language to facial expressions. Men are more likely to tune these cues out—the source of many male-female conflicts.

The male brain's floor plan, on the other hand, makes them naturally equipped at spatial relations and working with three-dimensional objects and drawings. On average, they also tend to score on the high end of math tests and are good at thinking analytically about abstract relationships and patterns.

To see these differences in action, let's take the classic scenario of a couple lost on a road trip. A man may be better at reading a map than a woman. But when there's no map on hand, women are better (and more willing) to reach out and *communicate* with another human being to ask for help. This doesn't mean women can't read maps, or men can't ask for directions. But our brains may make us privilege one activity over another: we tend to do what come easiest to us and what we think will get us the fastest results.

Women intuitively want to connect through dialogue and sharing. If your organization were to offer features that enabled them to talk with other like-minded individuals about your issue and unite behind a collective solution, they would thank you for bridging the connection. These positive associations would contribute to the vitality of your brand.

Women's Big Picture Thinking, or the Science on *Cultivate*

Various students have shown how gender differences affect the way men and women approach problem solving and decision making. Given a problem, a man's M.O. is to analyze, compartmentalize, and "attack" at key points in order to arrive at a solution. A woman, on the other hand, is more likely to insist on getting a full understanding of the *scope* of a problem by absorbing a great deal of information that weighs into her decision. This is the "tougher customer" principle in action. Generally speaking, she's more in tune to the interpersonal dynamics at play, whereas his approach is more like a precision instrument that relies on a more formulaic deduction. This is why when a woman complains about a problem at work or frustration with a family member, the male response is often to "cut to the chase" and go into active problem-solving mode, when, in fact, she needs him to walk and talk through with her all the different factors that are contributing to her unhappiness.

Enter: Hormones

Most women have a love-hate relationship with their hormones. They bristle when others point out that their menstrual cycles are affecting their thinking or behavior. But they're forced to acknowledge that hormonal changes do, in fact, affect how they think, perceive, and feel.

As it turns out, brains aren't everything. What's really behind gendered differences is the interplay between the male and female brain and hormones. During infantile puberty, baby girls get a two-year dose of estrogen, which has the effect of reinforcing women's predilection for social bonding and compromise. Boys, of course, get an extra shot of testosterone, which gives them the characteristics we frequently associate with maleness: aggressiveness and assertiveness, a strong competitive streak, and a stomach for risk-taking.

Sociolinguist Deborah Tannen describes talk between men and women as "cross-cultural communications" because we grow up in essentially different cultures ruled by our biological and social forces. For women, "life is a community, a struggle to preserve intimacy and avoid isolation. Hierarchies are more of friendship than of power." Conversely, men see things in terms of a hierarchy where they are either "one-up or one-down." Life, to men, "is a contest to preserve independence and avoid failure."

Remember our scenario about the woman who wanted her partner to listen and help her process her problems instead of diving straight into solution mode? As it turns out, we have hormones to thank for this female expectation, too. Brizendine calls oxytocin the "bonding hormone," which gets a boost from social contact and gets released when we feel stress. So when women feel crappy, their natural inclination is to reach out and connect with a friend so their oxytocin levels will shoot back up and return them to a sense of emotional equilibrium.

Harmonious Coop vs. Pecking Order, or the Science on *Community*

As we illustrated at the beginning of this chapter, these different orientations affect us from a very early age. When girls play, it's in the spirit of community and cooperation; studies show they "take turns" 20 times more often than boys. Boys' play is about the game itself, where the winner is the one who successfully defends his territory or proves his physical mettle. Lisa C.'s sister once told a funny story about her then-four-year-old daughter, who was waiting patiently to take a run down a slide at the local park, when a boy dressed in his Halloween costume blithely cut in front of her. Filled with an indomitable sense of order and purpose, the little girl stamped her foot and cried out, "It's *my* turn, Batman!"

Brizendine offers a provocative counter-theory to Summers' controversial speculation for why more women aren't represented in the fields of math and science. She suggests that it may be because pursuing these disciplines often involves many solitary hours in a laboratory, which lacks appeal for women, most of whom are drawn to more people-oriented careers.

Modern evolutionary theory put forth in seminal texts like Richard Dawkins's *The Selfish Gene* traces gendered behaviors to our roles as egg carriers and sperm givers. According to Dawkins, we are driven by the biological impulse to propagate our genes. For a woman, that means protecting her eggs at all costs. The female's goal is to stay alive and forge strong social ties ("It takes a village"). Hence, a woman's worldview tends to be dominated by a strong sense of interdependence—"we're all in this together." A woman's goal is to build consensus and smooth over conflict. For a man, it means "may the best sperm win." It's a man's job to be Alpha Monkey so he can beat out the competition and produce progeny. The male worldview is defined by battle, or "survival of the fittest."

Researchers in the field of psychological development have traced the influence of these gendered worldviews on how women and men make moral decisions. Studies show that the male approach to morality is defined by a strong sense of justice. For men, morality is self-oriented—don't infringe or interfere in the rights of others and protect your own rights. The female approach, on the other hand, is based on the idea that people have responsibilities for one another and doing the right thing means taking care of others. For them, acting in their own self-interest is morally wrong because it's selfish. Men care about the pecking order. Women care about keeping harmony in the coop. Given the problems facing our country and the world today, we need more than ever to call upon women's abilities to build and strengthen communities, a central theme of this book.

Conclusion

Not only do women and men have different plumbing, they're also wired differently, which has huge implications for how we appeal to them, win their trust, and move them to take action on behalf of our causes and our candidates. One marketing approach won't fit all. These gendered differences should compel us to question the bias of seemingly universal marketing efforts, and how many so-called gender neutral marketing tactics have in fact catered to men and alienated women in the process. It should also push us to think more deeply about the most effective ways to turn the dial up or down to get good reception from our target audiences, whether they're male or female.

In the next chapter we'll take on that age-old question, "What do women want?" The answers may surprise you.

Chapter Take-Aways

- Men and women are creatures of both biology and social conditioning, which produce fundamental differences that affect our perceptions, behaviors, and priorities. The better we understand these differences, the better we'll be at marketing for social good.

- Gender differences are not the same as gender equality. You can believe in gender differences yet full-heartedly support equality between men and women. Insisting that we live in a gender-blind society is as problematic as insisting we live in a color-blind one. Women's brains are wired differently from men's, which predisposes women to:

    — connect with other people through dialogue and sharing;

    — be better communicators and better at big-picture thinking; and

    — create community instead of hierarchy ("we"versus "me").

- One marketing approach doesn't fit all. Gender-based differences have huge implications for how we appeal to men and women, win their trust, and move them to take action.

3

What
Women
Want

Beyond Choice: Redefining "Women's Issues"

Not long ago, Lisa W. attended a fundraiser in New York City's Upper East Side for an aspiring candidate for president of the United States. At one point in the evening, she seized the opportunity to ask the candidate what issues he thought were important to her. He smiled and spent the next 15 minutes outlining his position on abortion.

The candidate gave the rap he thought he was supposed to give. He laid it on pink. Unfortunately, his answer was out of step with the time—but it wasn't entirely his fault. For years, choice has been front and center on the women's movement's agenda and its most politically influential organizations. This has been mutually reinforced by conservative groups and the religious right that have given abortion top billing in their "values"-driven debate. There's no denying that choice is a lightning rod issue, and that, for a notable number of Americans, it remains the single issue that determines their vote in electoral races.

But when it comes to defining so-called "women's issues," times have changed, and women with them. We live in a post-9/11 world, where the threat of terrorism on our own soil in addition to the wars we fight abroad have placed an enormous premium on national and international security and diplomacy. We live in a highly competitive global economy where manufacturing jobs—the type middle-class Americans once counted on to employ generations of their families—are becoming extinct, lured away by cheaper labor costs abroad. We live in an age where scientists tell us that we have, at most, eight to ten years to take decisive action on global warming, or face certain environmental catastrophe.

It used to be that political candidates could talk to female audiences about "soft" issues like education, health care, and yes, choice, and figure they had safely covered their bases. But this is no longer the case. Those issues are still close to women's hearts. But as the world evolves around us (and as women seize a larger piece of the economic pie and their family and civic responsibilities grow more varied and complex), the tent of women's concerns has grown much larger to encompass the military, jobs, and the economy—issues that have historically been deemed "male." As the country becomes increasingly shaped by the ascendant influence of women in the first decade of the 21st century, it follows that there are few issues that are *not* "women's issues" precisely because the definition of women's issues is evolving; there are few if any areas in society today which do not affect women personally, politically, practically—or all of the above.

It's not as though men and women care about completely separate issues. It's simply that women actually care about all the same things men do—and even more. Men care about national security and defense. Women care about these too, along with affordable health care and quality education. Political candidates who worry about alienating men by focusing on so-called women's issues have their priorities misplaced. They would be more successful if they paid more attention to hitting the She Spot by meeting women's much higher threshold. In other words, once you ditch the misconception of women as a niche audience, you become, overall, a more effective marketing expert for reaching all your audiences.

The Rule of the Four Cs

If you want women on your side, you may have to re-wire and update your thinking about what it is that they want. Given that unmarried women have been identified as the "number one 'get'" for candidates in the 2008 elections, the time is ripe to do this work.

We've come up with four principles to keep in mind as you formulate an effective marketing strategy to reach women:

1. Care

2. Connect

3. Cultivate

4. Control

Women *care* about transforming society for the better, and want more *control* over their lives. They also want to *connect* and to *cultivate* other like-minded people into a larger and more powerful force for change.

1. Care
(can't leave home without it)

Nurturant mother vs. Strict father

So what do women want? There are several ways of getting at the answer to this question. Rather than leap immediately to a nuts-and-bolts discussion about women's political priorities, it's worth taking a step back to examine the general worldviews that color our political thinking, and where women fall on that spectrum.

Many readers of this book are likely to have some passing familiarity with the work of George Lakoff, a linguistics professor at the University of California, Berkeley, whose seminal book, *Moral Politics* and the more recent *Don't Think of an Elephant* have helped push the Democratic Party and progressive organizations to pay closer attention to how they frame their issues and political positions to gain greater mainstream appeal.

At the heart of Lakoff's thinking is his characterization of progressive and conservative worldviews as "nurturant mother" and "strict father," respectively. In short, the progressive worldview assumes that the world is basically good and can be made even better. This concept extends to children with parents who model inspiring behavior and teach them to be morally aware human beings who "do good unto others as you would have done unto you." The primary virtues in this nurturing system are empathy and responsibility. In the progressive's mind, the government's role is to protect its citizens with social safety nets and regulations from outside threat.

In contrast, the conservative worldview is based on the "strict father" model, which perceives the world as dangerous and difficult. Children are born misbehaving and must be taught right from wrong. Under this model, the strict father is the moral authority who supports and defends the family. "Good" people are those who possess the strengths of self-discipline and self-reliance. These good citizens effectively earn the wealth and political power ceded to them, and are in the position to impose a similar sense of discipline onto others. The government's role is to maintain order and administer justice. Social safety-net programs are devalued because they coddle people by handing to them things they haven't earned.

So how do these two contrasting worldviews jibe with gendered worldviews?

Not surprisingly, when we match Lakoff's definitions with the wealth of research that's been done on how women construct and view the world, we find that women are inclined to hold the nurturant mother worldview.

These differences can be traced directly into the wiring of our brains. A number of landmark studies have revealed how men and women think differently when confronted with issues of power, ethics, personal aspirations, and self-perception. For example, for men, power traditionally consists of "domination and aggression." For women, however, power is something more subtle: it's "the force that creates relationships, binds families and builds societies."

In *Brain Sex: The Real Difference Between Men and Women*, Anne Moir and David Jessel describe a study that asked male and female subjects how they would approach a theoretical moral dilemma: A man's wife is dying. He can't afford the drug that could save her life. Should the man steal the drug?

> The men saw it as a simple matter of justice—what was the right thing to do. The women asked other questions based on the principle of caring—what was the responsible thing to do. Couldn't the man discuss the matter with the pharmacist? Couldn't he borrow the money? What would happen to his wife if he were caught stealing the drug and sent to prison? The questions the women raised showed that they perceived different dimensions to a problem, including the moral aspect, theft; they may come up with a less snappy answer, but it is almost certainly a more comprehensive one.

In other words, a woman is predisposed to apply her "big picture" brain to the problem by making sure all the potential ramifications of a given action are understood, whereas a man is inclined to get in and get out based on a core conviction.

Research that probes the personal aspirations of men and women sheds additional light.

In an oft-cited survey of six modern cultures, men and women were asked to describe the "kind of person I would most like to be." Men identified the following characteristics for their ideal selves: practical, shrewd, assertive, dominating, competitive, critical, self-controlled. Women, on the other hand, zeroed in on a set of very different criteria: loving, affectionate, impulsive, sympathetic, and generous.

In a separate survey commissioned by the Leukemia & Lymphoma Society, women were asked to rank what they wanted to accomplish during their lifetime. The respondents overwhelmingly chose "help make someone else's life better" above other possibilities on their "to-do list" including "be my own boss" and "travel to exciting places." These findings are in line with an earlier study conducted by Gray Advertising, which found that women ranked "make the world a better place" higher than other aspirations including "accumulate wealth" or "be really successful in my career."

Taken together, these gender differences suggest that women have a strong nurturing streak. Given women's traditional role as mothers, it may seem like a no-brainer that their concept of self and life priorities more mirror the progressive nurturant parent than the strict father model. Women are more likely to take into account the push-pull of extenuating circumstances (think empathy and responsibility) than to see things in stark black and white terms. The implications for progressives and nonprofit organizations are clear: the lines between what women want and progressive social change goals are connected at their core. The remainder of this book is dedicated to helping you maximize these natural fault lines with greater effectiveness.

Keeping the Faith

No discussion of what women want would be complete without touching on what they *believe*. A dominant theme of the 2004 election was the important role that evangelicals played in sending George W. Bush to the White House. But beyond that election—and beyond evangelicals as a religious group—faith has come to influence increasingly not only the values by which many Americans live daily, but also those values by which they make their voting decisions. These trends, according to Lake and Conway, are driven by women, "the guardians of the soul."

In a recent Gallup poll, 83 percent of women over 50 and 65 percent of women under 50 rated religion as "extremely important" at significantly higher rates than men. In the 2004 election, 43% of women voters reported attending religious services a few times a week or more. Our nation may have separation of religion and state, but the lines may not be so simple in the minds of voters. This is a reality that progressives have gradually come to understand.

In raising this issue, we do not mean to suggest that nonprofit organizations should take to invoking God in their direct mail campaigns. But we do mean that they should be conscious of how progressive values overlap with religious values, and how to make the most of this overlap.

For example, members of religious groups readily make time in their busy lives to volunteer at soup kitchens and otherwise give back to charities that help the homeless and others less fortunate than themselves. These acts of giving are deeply ingrained in the Christian, Jewish, and Muslim faiths, as well as many other popular mainstream religions. Yet many of the same people who give so selflessly as direct-service volunteers draw the line at advocating for social policies that could help reduce the ranks of the "needy" at soup kitchens and homeless shelters.

The conservative right does not have a monopoly on people of faith. Until now, they've just been better at rallying the troops. The challenge for those of us who work on behalf of progressive policy change is to find fruitful ways of bridging the gap between the spiritual and the political.

Change: A Women's Political Agenda for the 21st Century

Every election year, presidential hopefuls line up to compete for the title of "change candidate."

They would do well to appeal to the single largest group of "change voters": women—specifically unmarried women.

Single women—a group that includes never-marrieds as well as divorced and widowed women—voted for change in larger numbers than any other group in the 2006 election, which resulted in Democrats taking back Congress for the first time in a dozen years. For women, change remains the defining characteristic of their political agenda going into the 2008 election as well, according to a January 2007 national survey of unmarried women by Women's Voices. Women Vote.

This was true across every major issue, from wanting an exit strategy to get out of Iraq to wanting wholesale reform to make healthcare coverage available and affordable for all. Tellingly, only seven percent of the women polled named "preserve a woman's right to choose" as their top priority for what they want Congress to achieve over the next two years.

"These women want America to head in a new direction, both at home and abroad, and they want a leader that will take it there," said Page Gardner, founder and president of Women's Voices. Women Vote. "They seek an end to the Iraq war. They want a raise in the minimum wage and pay equity so they can support their families."

We see this desire and willingness to transform the status quo reflected in charitable giving, with women more likely than men to donate to organizations they believe are shaking things up by changing the systems or root causes of so many of society's ills.

Yet single women's drive for change has not translated at the polls, where they have historically not voted in proportion to their numbers. As we'll discuss in greater detail in Chapter 6, part of the problem lies with the fact that single women, more than other groups, do not perceive politicians as an effective conduit to making change, which is exacerbated by the fact that most politicians have not done a good job of listening to single women or speaking to them about issues that matter most to them. In our view, these patterns point to an incredible opportunity for political campaigns to engage this key voting bloc for the upcoming and future elections.

2. Connect
(winning her support begins with earning her trust)

As research for this book, we talked to a Democratic fundraiser friend of ours about her experience cultivating female donors. She confessed that, for the most part, she didn't bother because it took considerably more investment on her part to convince women to open their pocketbooks—if they opened them at all. She made a calculated decision that it literally wasn't worth her time. "Women take too long," she said.

Our friend was right about one thing: When it comes to signing checks, women are traditionally slower to act than men. Part of the reason is because, in general, women take more time to make up their mind on virtually everything. They're the ones you see at the supermarket scrutinizing the long list of ingredients on a jar of spaghetti sauce. They deliberate longer in the dressing room, ticking through a check-list in their minds: *Will this blouse match the other clothes in my closet? Does it make me look like I'm trying to look younger than I am? Is it too casual to wear at work, or can I get away with it?* Similarly, women think long and hard about household purchases like cell phone plans and personal computers because they have to run through a universe of possible scenarios for use balanced against everything else in their lives, including a partner and children.

In other words, for women, the devil is in the details: each decision involves several dimensions that must be considered. For men, decision-making is a much more calculated and even formulaic process. These gendered approaches to decision-making carry over into the realm of (political and philanthropic) giving, too.

According to public opinion expert Celinda Lake, "Women want to know more about the personal background of the candidate. They also want to know about the values that led to the political position the candidate has taken. The personal is political for women. Men, on the other hand, are likely to say, 'Just tell me your top three policies.'"

Yet, aside from how long it takes for women to make up their minds, the reality is, at least for now, once they have made up their minds, women are less inclined to give to political candidates than men are.

So when it comes to women's giving, what gives? To get to the bottom of this question, the Women's Campaign Forum Foundation, a Washington, DC-based organization committed to engaging more women in politics with a special focus on women political donors, conducted a series of focus groups in the winter of 2007. The results were eye-opening.

Women, in fact, do give. But compared to their track record on political donations, they are more likely to give to nonprofit organizations, which they trust are taking direct action on the issues that matter to them most. Generally speaking, they have less faith in politicians, and in the political process, to be as effective as agents of change.

A side effect of this skepticism is that, while many young women volunteer, only half of them voted in the 2004 election. It's worth noting, however, that more women than men ages 18–24 went to polls in the last presidential election, and that overall, the young voters turn-out in 2004 represented a significant spike compared to previous years. Time will tell if this is a one-time phenomenon or an indication of a larger trend. Studies on young women's political giving show that the majority of them say they don't feel politics contributes to their lives or to changing the world. High-profile political scandals in their lifetime—from the Monica Lewinsky affair to the false reports of weapons of mass destruction that led to the invasion of Iraq—may well have contributed to this poor, blanket impression. We would argue, too, that lack of targeted marketing to their demographic has something to do with the fact that many young women stay home on election day. Whatever the reason (and there is surely more than one reason), the surprising truth remains: these twenty-somethings, who more than any previous generation have been raised to assert themselves and to go after what they want in their professional and personal lives, are not translating their sense of personal power to political power.

The negative perception of politics among women both young and old may also be colored by the relative lack of female candidates in national election campaigns (the good news is, more than 80 percent of Americans say they are ready for a female president). Yet the same does not seem to hold true at the local level. More and more women are running for seats on school boards, on city councils, and in state legislatures, where they feel they can make a difference closer to home.

With Nancy Pelosi ascending to Speaker of the House, and with the increasing presence of women in Congress thanks to a number of political upsets in the 2006 midterm election, we may see a shift in women's perception of and confidence in leaders in higher office. That said, it is worth noting as untrue the assumption that women will automatically favor a female candidate over her male competitor. Women have proven themselves to be more agenda-conscious than gender-conscious. Female candidates who run on traditional women's issues like education and health care alone can no longer count on the female vote. A recent study by the nonprofit White House Project showed that voters also wanted to see women candidates take a strong position on national security and against terrorism, and favored messages that advocated for an approach that combined a strong military with international diplomacy.

Another important theme that emerged from this area of research was that, when it comes to making social change, women say they want to feel part of a movement, to be connected to something larger than themselves. It's less important to them to be the biggest donor in the room and more important to feel they are contributing side-by-side with others, accumulating power through numbers.

This finding is echoed in Sondra C. Shaw and Martha A. Taylor's book, *Reinventing Fundraising: Realizing the Potential of Women's Philanthropy*. When it comes to the "personal reward" that women receive from their philanthropy, the women the authors talked to said the value they got from acts of altruism was a "sense of self-empowerment" and the "reward of feeling part of a larger community." As one woman said, "By giving to an organization I support, I am also empowering myself to be part of that organization and carry on its value system."

Again, when it comes to political contributions, women are wary of a certain impurity of "self interest" that they find counter to their stronger desire to give in a more "selfless" way that would make the world a better place.

The lesson here is two-fold: One, if you're a political campaigner who wants women in your camp, you first must connect with them by winning their trust and overcoming their skepticism about politics-as-usual. Two, you should think creatively about how to tap into women's desire to feel connected to other people who share similar ideals and beliefs.

3. Cultivate (strength in numbers)

To review: women are less likely to give to political candidates than men are, *and,* when they do give, they tend to give less. It begs the $100 million question: *Why bother?*

Because there's more than one way to raise $100 million dollars.

According to Allison Fine, author of *Momentum: Igniting Social Change in the Connected Age*, men are more likely than women to cut a fat $20,000 check. But size isn't everything.

It may take more effort to bring women on board, but it's worth the pay-off for two reasons. The first is the power of word of mouth. If you cultivate the support of two women to donate $1,000 each and then inspire them to tell eight more friends about it (and so on, and so on) you hit the same $10,000 jackpot and you've seeded your message among many more potential donors. The second reason involves the "tougher customer" principle. Women will scrutinize everything before they decide whether they're in or they're out, but once they're in, they tend to be extremely loyal and committed to your cause. This is because they've done the work of poking and prodding to their satisfaction and decided you passed the test. Once you've passed—you're in. To paraphrase marketing guru Faith Popcorn, "Women don't buy brands; they join them." What's more, she encourages businesses to connect women to each other as a marketing strategy for connecting them to a company's brand. We'll discuss this idea further in Chapter 5.

Fundraisers miss golden opportunities for seed capital when they limit their prospects to big-dollar funders and neglect smaller donors who could, in the end, bring in bigger fish, more fish, and fish you may not have had the right bait for on your own.

Fine's advice: "Build larger bases of smaller and medium-sized donors and stop genuflecting in front of the $100,000 donors." The fact that the election cycle now appears to kick off earlier and last longer has created the ideal conditions for cultivating women's support. There's more time to appeal to the tough customer in them, and once they're on board, more time to see your initial investment grow when they start tapping their own personal and professional networks on your behalf.

Cultivate Her and You Get Him, Too

As we described briefly in Chapter 1, when you market to women effectively by listening to what they want and meeting what they need, you not only gain their support, you gain the support of men, too.

Why? It's not that men are simpler life forms than women. It's that they tend to look at things more directly, without accounting for as many "what ifs" as women do.

Remember the check-list in the dressing room? When women make decisions, they run through an exhaustive list of inputs and variables. For the most part, men are content to stick with the basics—although, of course, there are exceptions to the rule. But generally speaking, when you meet women's higher, "tougher customer" threshold, you'll sail above the men's bar as well and bring them along with you.

In other words, while men will settle for a simple cup of joe, women may ask for half-decaf with skim milk, get a few cookies for her coworkers, and order a salad for later so she can use her lunch hour to schedule her kids' doctor appointments and call her mom. Women are often thinking about the big picture, and they're also thinking two steps into the future. Just stand in line at any Starbucks and you can see that they get this.

Because men have traditionally been the measure of all things, women have been met only partway. So, as Carol Tavris points out, when Congress and the United Nations raise concerns about the international violations of human rights, these violations have rarely included violations of women's rights such as genital mutilation, forced prostitution, domestic violence, or a host of other conditions that relegate women to second-class status in society. Likewise, when we talk about workforce and job stimulation initiatives, we don't match them with an affordable daycare plan so women will not be caught in the financial Catch-22 of wanting or needing to earn more money, but having the cost of daycare defeat the purpose of putting in more hours.

4. Control
(putting her in the driver's seat)

Calgon, take me away...

You may remember this line from a TV commercial that ran in the 1980s for Calgon bath powder. In the ad spot, a housewife becomes increasingly frazzled as a dog tracks mud on the carpet, her children make a mess, and dinner burns on the stove. Just as the phone rings, she cries out the famous line and is immediately transported to an escapist bubble bath.

Flash forward more than 20 years later, and it's a much different picture. Women still live incredibly busy lives, whether they work at home, on the job, or, as is often the case, both. Yet ask women, regardless of their income or marital status, and the majority of them will tell you that there's never been a better time to be a woman. So if they're looking for anything, it's not escape. They want *control*.

Women today acknowledge that their lives are a juggling act, but they're proud of their ability to keep all the balls in the air. In most households, women may clock-in the same number of hours on the job as their male partners, but come home and do the larger share of the cooking, cleaning, and grocery shopping. An increasing number of "sandwich" generation women have also found themselves assuming responsibility not only for their children's care but for their aging parents' care as well.

Last year the Columbia School of Journalism sponsored a panel titled, "What Do Women Want?" The panelists, all news media professionals, were asked to give their answer to what they thought women want from their news sources.

Geralyn Lucas, director of public affairs for the Lifetime Network and author of *Why I Wore Lipstick to My Mastectomy*, answered, "Honesty and authenticity. When you're honest, you have credibility. We're seeing more of that in the media. A good babysitter. Good filters for what's true and what's not."

Lynn Povich of the International Women's Media Foundation answered the question this way: "Why are we still asking this question? Women want complete equality. They want the same things men want: news on Iraq, news on DC, how to understand their husband and where to buy a good pair of shoes."

These two women were speaking to their industry, the news media. But their answers also naturally threw in the hodge-podge of demands and priorities that make up the complex fabric of their lives as women—children, husbands, and yes, shoes.

So while women are keeping the balls in the air, they also want to live life on a slower track—what Lake and Conway dub the "mouse race." According to research by these two public opinion pollsters, the biggest challenge facing young women—the 20 percent of the female population ages 20–40—is life-work balance, including managing child-rearing with their professional lives. Lucas, a Gen-Xer, was actually late for the panel because she had trouble lining up a sitter that evening.

Nonprofit organizations and political candidates who can speak to these pressures and offer relief will get an open ear from women. Americans today—especially women—are starved for time. They want more time to spend with family, more time to exercise and take care of their health, and more time to focus on their passions outside work. Even if you don't work on an issue that will directly help them with this no-time dilemma, there are still ways you can make their lives easier if you make your "ask" in the right way.

"Women want the 'two-for,'" according to Lake. "They want more than one thing because they are pressed for time and want the 'value add.'"

In Chapter 7, we will take a closer look at how nonprofit organizations have successfully appealed to their target audiences by delivering this two-for.

Conclusion

Most women agree that there has never been a better time to be a woman. At the same time, they will also tell you they're not satisfied with the direction the country is going—and that they're more than ready to invest in change. These views are not as contradictory as they may appear on first glance. Indeed, they speak to the very reasons women make such a powerful instrument for change.

Women today are filled with optimism and hope for the future. Part of women's hope is grounded in a growing sense of their own power and of the hard-won gains they've made in society. But they're not willing to rest on their laurels, nor do they want the world to, not when there is so much more work to be done. In the following pages, we'll discuss how to tap these complementary forces and harness them for social transformation.

Chapter Take-Aways

- If you want women on your side, you may have to re-wire and update your thinking about what they want. Women *care* and they want more *control* over their lives. They also want to *connect* and *cultivate* other like-minded people into a larger and more powerful force for change.

- The lines between what women want and progressive social change goals are connected at their core.

- While women may take longer to cultivate as donors and supporters, once they're on board, they tend to be more loyal and more effective word-of-mouth foot soldiers.

Women's optimism and "can do" attitude, combined with their restless desire for change, make them an ideal audience for organizations working for social transformation.

Part II

How to
Hit the
She Spot

4

Care

The Nonprofit that Knew Too Much

The very first step to getting people to support your cause is getting them to care. Most of us in the nonprofit world got into this line of work because we care. We care about keeping our air and oceans free of pollution. We care about improving education and leveling the playing field for low-income kids. We care about protecting our right to free speech.

But sometimes a funny thing happens on our way to making the world a better place. The deeper we get into our issues and the better experts we become, the worse we get at communicating with our audiences. We start dropping cryptic acronyms and technical terms. Giant pandas and blue whales become "charismatic mega-fauna." Statistics replace human beings. We get so caught up explaining the complexities of our issues that we neglect to convey the passion that drove us to do this work in the first place, which is our best bet for convincing others to join us. We worry about "dumbing down" our message for the masses, when, in fact, what they want from us is plainer speak. In short, we become the Nonprofit that Knew Too Much.

When it comes to marketing your cause, you don't need to be the smartest person in the room. Communications professionals in our business will often talk about "reaching hearts and minds." But a more useful rephrasing may be, "Reach hearts first, before appealing to the mind." Most people are motivated to take action because their emotions have been triggered, not because they've analyzed a cost-benefit spreadsheet or have seen the logic in doing good. This chapter is about making sure the principle of caring is at the center of your marketing efforts.

Who Cares? Women Do.

Creating an emotional bond between your issue and your target audience is especially important when that audience is women. When you tickle a woman's empathy bone, you make a powerful connection you can then translate into fundraising dollars, activism, and word-of-mouth support.

A woman's predilection for empathy—her "soft spot" if you will—begins at the cradle.

Studies have shown that baby girls less than two days old are more likely to respond to the cries of another baby and to the human face than baby boys. In *The Female Brain,* Brizendine attributes this ability to a hormone-charged period known as "infantile puberty," which lasts only 9 months for boys but 24 months for girls. During this phase, the female infant's ovaries produce huge amounts of estrogen that "marinate" her brain. This helps develop the ovaries, but it also helps develop brain neurons that sharpen their powers of observation, communications, tending, and caring.

These differences continue to play out in childhood. Compared to boys, girls are better judges when it comes to gauging whether they are hurting someone's feelings. They're also better at "reading" the feelings of a character in a story, a process known as "emotional mirroring." Brain-imaging studies have shown how observing or imagining another person's emotional state can automatically activate similar brain patterns in the person who is observing—and that these triggers are especially active among women. A woman's heightened sensitivity to emotional interplay and relationship dynamics makes her a natural and powerful ally for both recognizing and righting injustice. Smart marketing can help ensure that you harness these heightened senses in service of your organization and issues.

Getting Her to Care: Six Marketing Tips

If you watch ads aimed at male audiences (for example, for certain brands of cars, video games, and athletic shoes), the name of the game is *best,* whether it's the fastest, shiniest, or most turbo-charged. Men are driven by competition and the desire to be top of the heap. Savvy corporate marketing pros have learned that what works for men won't necessarily work for women. They apply what they've learned about the brain and behavioral differences we've described in the section above to tailor their marketing to appeal to women.

As Marti Barletta observes, "Women don't particularly want to be looked up to any more than they want to be looked down on. In the world of women, the ideal position is side by side. For women, the operative emotion is not envy, but empathy."

Nonprofits, too, can tap into this operative emotion to market social change. Below are six practical tips that speak particularly to women, but can resonate with men as well.

1. Put a face on your organization.

2. Keep it simple—and real.

3. Tell real-life stories.

4. Don't leave out the details.

5. Appeal to group affiliations.

6. Tickle her funny bone.

1. Put a face on your organization.

In our years of working with nonprofits, we've noticed a marked reluctance among more than a few professionals in the sector to promote a leader or leaders as the face of their organization. This was especially true among groups led by women that work explicitly on women's issues. The reasons for this usually fall into two categories:

- They worry the organization will become over-identified with a few individuals who may eventually leave.

- They're concerned that ceding the limelight to one person or a selected few will undercut contributions of the other staff.

We're sympathetic to these concerns, but they run counter to effective marketing. We are not advocating for organizations that turn themselves into "cult of personalities." But we *are* advocating for organizations that are guided by strong, visible leaders with a voice that is authentic and real.

Having an authentic voice, out front, is especially important in today's age of celebrity and personality. Beyond that, it's human nature to identify with individuals, not a faceless, monolithic organization. This is especially pertinent in today's high-tech era, where communications has become increasingly depersonalized. Just ask anyone who has had to slog through automated options in order to reach an actual human being on a 1-800 customer service line, or yearned for a sympathetic ear when dealing with a ticketing agency or credit card company.

For women who thrive on personal connections, interacting with a faceless entity can be especially off-putting. It also doesn't inspire trust. Well before automated phone systems, of course, advertising firms were creating signature personalities and characters to brand products and forge warm-fuzzy associations with the customer, from Mrs. Butterworth to Mr. Peanut.

In the 1980s, Ernest & Julio Gallo Winery went so far as to invent the folksy duo of Frank Bartles and Ed Jaymes to plug its line of Bartles and Jaymes wine coolers. The two elderly men (played by actors) talked directly to their customers from a front porch, punctuating each dispatch with the tagline, "Thank you for your support." The characters helped give the product a personable dimension that customers could relate to.

The good news for nonprofits is that most are not so monolithic or bureaucratic that it would be difficult to put a personal foot—or face—forward. But doing so requires a commitment to promoting and more closely identifying a leader or leaders as the public face of the organization. The gains—more intimacy and trust with your audiences—far outweigh the concerns we described earlier. Give people credit for understanding that nonprofits experience turn-over like anywhere else. In the same vein, recognize that people need to see leaders at the helm of any organization or company so they feel deeper connection and trust in knowing that thoughtful, caring human beings are calling the shots and looking out for the interests they care about.

Nonprofit Case Study: **The People Behind MoveOn.org**

An organization that we think does an effective job of personalizing their communications is MoveOn.org. The advocacy group was founded by husband and wife Wes Boyd and Joan Blades, Bay Area software entrepreneurs who invented the flying toasters screensaver. The year was 1998. Boyd and Blades were frustrated with the partisan warfare surrounding the Monica Lewinsky controversy and wanted politicians in DC to redirect their focus to more important national affairs. Hence the catch phrase, "move on" was born.

What started as an online petition sent to just a hundred of their friends and family grew within one week to reach a hundred thousand people. Blades, who calls herself an "accidental activist," described what happened next: "At that point, we thought it was going to be a flash campaign, that we would help everyone connect with leadership in all the ways we could figure out, and then get back to our regular lives. A half a million people ultimately signed and we somehow never got back to our regular lives."

MoveOn.org has since grown to 3.3 million members, taking on issues ranging from gun safety to campaign finance reform. But it was the Iraq War that would truly solidify the Internet advocacy group's standing as a major political force. As part of the Win Without War coalition, which included the National Council of Churches, the NAACP, and NOW, MoveOn.org helped drive mass petitions and street protests and raised millions of dollars to pay for anti-war advertising campaigns.

Despite being a largely virtual enterprise, they kept their communications intimate with small but important touches, like personally signing their E-action alerts with "Wes," "Joan," or "Eli" (MoveOn PAC Executive Director Eli Pariser). They made every $35 donor feel like part of something bigger and more powerful. In doing so, they tapped into a segment of the population that wanted to make a difference, but found it difficult to get a foothold in traditional political campaigns or with nonprofits that asked for their money, but didn't necessarily engage or empower their commitment in other ways.

It Takes a Nation

One the most dramatic outcomes of MoveOn.org's brand of intimate, people-to-people organizing was www.HurricaneHousing.org, a rapid response campaign founded to match survivors of Hurricane Katrina with volunteers offering temporary shelter in their own homes.

Executive Director Eli Pariser remembered having second thoughts about whether such an effort would work. He worried that most Americans, inundated with crime reports on TV, would be wary of letting strangers into their home. But the need was too great not to try. "We went ahead anyway," he recalled. "What else could we do? Getting people into safe housing had to be our first priority."

Within five hours of the first email appeal to MoveOn.org members, a few thousand people had offered rooms for disaster victims to stay, from a college student in Starkville, Mississippi to a family in Navarre, Florida who added that there was a public school near their house for evacuated children. By next morning, the number of offers had exceeded the 8,000 mark. A toll-free hotline was created so evacuees could "search" the listings by phone.

In the end, the effort paired more than 30,000 evacuees with people who opened their homes. A number of their stories were collected in a book, *It Takes a Nation: How Strangers Became Family in the Wake of Hurricane Katrina* (Palace Press International, 2006). In the foreword, Sen. Barack Obama wrote of the "surge of empathy" that drove thousands of Americans to host people rendered homeless by the hurricane was proof of the country's "capacity for greatness." The oral histories collected in the book, he continued, "show everyday heroes at work" and the "power this online community has to strengthen our national community, and calls each of us to do what we can to follow this heartfelt example."

Sierra Mohawk of Stone Mountain, Georgia housed Michelle Peterson and Dennis Scott, who spent seven days in the Superdome and then two weeks at a military base in Oklahoma before connecting with Mohawk.

"To me, it was natural to take in Dennis and Michelle," Mohawk said. "I come from a really big family. When you have a family crisis and someone loses their apartment and they've got five kids, you learn how to live with those situations. I'm the oldest of nine children. So we're used to big numbers."

MoveOn's active membership base wasn't born overnight. But their success supports the idea that you can build a cadre of loyal and highly engaged members when you create an organization that makes people feel *emotionally* invested, both in the people who run the organization as human beings, and in their fellow members, who have banded together because they share similar ideals about social progress. In Chapter 5 we'll revisit MoveOn.org by focusing more on its community of members as a force for activism.

2. Keep it simple—and real.

At Fenton Communications, one of the services we offer to our clients is a process called "messaging and positioning." The process is designed to help nonprofit organizations refine and define the space they occupy in the minds of their target audiences and to differentiate them-selves from their peers and competitors (think "Mac" vs. "PC").

As part of the positioning process, we ask nonprofit staff and other stakeholders to answer a series of questions. One of them is: "How would you describe what you do to a 12-year-old?"

Our goal here is not to get people to dumb it down, nor do we mean to suggest that Americans won't "get it" unless we talk to them like children. The goal is to get our clients to strip away excess information and professional jargon to get at the *core*. This is why newspapers are written at a sixth- or fifth-grade reading level. It doesn't mean reporters are writing for people who never made it to high school. But they are using language that emphasizes clarity and simplicity, with a minimum of abstraction, so readers can fluidly come away with the substance and meaning of the story.

Posing the "12-year-old challenge" often has a radical effect on our clients. The same individuals, who earlier in the survey had described their work in soulless nonprofit- and foundation-speak, strip away the jargon to reveal the heart beating at the center of what they do.

Here are two examples of what we're talking about. We asked the staff at a nonprofit that provides loans to low-income, small-business entrepreneurs to describe in a sentence what they do. Here's how a few of them responded:

> *A nonprofit organization that provides financial products and services that enable people to develop financial independence and self-sufficiency.*

> *A nonprofit microfinance institute that helps low-income communities build assets.*

When we asked the staff to answer the same question as if they were talk-ing to a 12-year-old, their answers were much different:

> *We help people who have little money start small businesses or buy a home by lending them money. We help people help themselves.*

> *We help hardworking people make a better life for themselves by providing loans to help them grow their businesses and teaching them how to save and manage their business better.*

Guess which versions ended up on the cutting-room floor and which ones became the basis for organizational messaging.

Here's another example, this time involving a center that provides integrative medicine to patients. We asked the staff to describe what they do. One person responded:

> *We conduct scientifically rigorous research into complementary and alternative therapies, educate medical students, practitioners, and the public about these therapies and establish a clinical practice that provides medical care integrating Western-style "scientific" medicine with complementary and alternative therapies.*

Whew.

But here's a typical response we got when we asked staff members to explain the same thing to a 12-year-old:

> *The center is a place where people who have health issues or who want to feel better come to get treatment that they may not get from their regular doctor. They learn new ways to help themselves, like taking yoga or getting acupuncture, or learning to eat better to take care of themselves.*

Without the 12-year-old audience in mind, nonprofits will often describe *what* they do instead of *why* they do it and *who* stands to benefit. Yet it's the *who* and *why* that really moves people. So the next time someone asks you at a party what you do for living, try this trick: Answer as though you were talking to a 12-year-old. Or, answer the question as though you had been asked *why* you do what you do for living. You may find yourself instinctively avoiding the insider lingo and vague buzz words that block clear communications.

3. Tell real-life stories.

Public interest communications expert Andy Goodman begins his guide for nonprofits, *Storytelling as Best Practice*, with this golden rule in public speaking: "In a two-hour speech, people will remember a two-minute story."

That's because human beings are "hardwired" to respond to stories, according to Goodman. We understand how the world works through narrative. A good *anecdote* is the best *antidote* to turgid statistics and abstract principles. This is because the best stories have built-in tension or conflict that sustains our interest; heroes and villains that capture our

---

Voting for the Candidate Who Cares

President Bill Clinton was famous for his ability to connect with ordinary Americans. When he said, "I feel your pain," we believed him. This empathetic quality—or lack thereof, can make or break a political candidacy.

Mitt Romney (and John Kerry before him) learned this the hard way in his bid for the Republican Presidential nomination. Covering a campaign pit stop in small-town Iowa, the *New York Times* described an encounter between Romney and the father of an Army National Guardsman about to leave for Iraq. The man asked the former governor of Massachusetts what his plan was for Iraq.

Romney's response was to dive right into eight minutes' worth of talking points that covered everything from praising the overthrow of Saddam Hussein to criticizing the Democrats' negative portrayal of the war. What he didn't do was acknowledge the man's fears that his son could be killed. The man walked away unimpressed, and the article went on to question whether Romney could "connect with voters," many of whom described him as "impressive but somewhat detached."

Much has been made about the importance Americans place on voting for the candidate they can imagine having a beer with. We want assurances they can hear us, see where we're coming from, and identify with our concerns. We want our leaders to lead. But at the end of the day, we need them to care.

---

imagination; and a resolution that supplies us with a window on the world, or on how we want our world to be.

Corporate marketing pros recognize that stories are particularly useful for reaching women because women shop with their imagination. They run scenarios in their minds of where and how the products will fit into their lives and how they'll interact with them. As marketing expert Tom Peters puts it, "Men want the headlines, the top line points," but women "require immersion in the whole experience of that product. She needs real sense of context."

Unfortunately, nonprofits often neglect to tell compelling stories that would help immerse their audiences into their issue and compel them to take action. By leaving out the nuts-and-bolts context of how their issues affect real people, nonprofits are missing out on a highly effective channel for reaching women in particular.

"Most progressive organizations are still focusing on very specific public policy change. The agenda is often developed by policy wonks and not placed in the larger context of people's lives," said Douglas Gould, founder and principal of Douglas Gould and Company, a communications consulting firm for nonprofits and foundations.

Below are two examples, one from the business sector and one from the nonprofit sector, that show how companies and nonprofits are using storytelling as a marketing tactic.

Corporate Case Study: **In Every Project There's a Story to Tell**

We opened this book with an account of how Home Depot has transformed its stores to meet today's market reality: women undertake nearly half of all do-it-yourself improvement projects at home. Home Depot's current "True Stories" marketing campaign offers another example of its female-friendly approach. The motto of the campaign, "In every project there's a story to tell," says it all. In commercials, print ads, and the company's Web site are real-life stories of customers who have used Home Depot products and training courses to tackle their own home improvement projects.

There's the story of Jan and Mike, a young couple who are adopting and wanted to fix up their bathroom—laying down new linoleum and replacing the toilet—before bringing their baby home. The transformation was so successful they're now thinking of installing a Jacuzzi tub in their other bathroom. Then there's Malaika, who had a childhood dream of owning a restaurant. She made it happen by building the "Brown Sack," a soup, sandwich, and shake shack, in just six months.

By focusing on the human benefits of their merchandise through storytelling, Home Depot accomplishes two tasks: one, they showcase the warm bond they have with their many satisfied customers; and two, they convince would-be customers that they, too, can tackle similar projects at home by demonstrating the successes of individuals, who, like us, may have limited skills with a hammer and nail.

Nonprofit Case Study: **Nothing Will Ever Be the Same**

The number one preventable cause of death in New York City is smoking. Cigarettes kill 9,000 New Yorkers a year. That's an average of more than 25 people a day.

In this day and age, you'd be hard pressed to find someone who isn't aware that smoking can kill you. Studies show that most smokers want to quit. But facts and stats alone weren't breaking through. The New York

Health Department knew it would have to try another tactic to stop people from lighting up.

They found one in Ronaldo Martinez.

Martinez, who lost his voice to throat cancer when he was 39 years old, is the star of a series of public service announcements that the Health Department started running on TV in 2006. In one ad, Martinez walks along a pool deck watching children at play and says in a mechanized voice, "I never thought that anything could keep me from the water. Now I have to breathe through a hole in my throat. If water gets inside of me, it will drown me." In the first year of the campaign, the Health Department reported receiving 15,000 calls to its toll-free hotline for would-be quitters, compared to 5,000 calls during the same period the year before.

In Martinez, the Health Department found a compelling protagonist whose real-life, daily struggles living with the consequences of smoking forced people to put themselves in his shoes. It was a much more unsettling place to be than in the land of Surgeon General warnings.

4. Don't leave out the details.

When Lisa W. was looking for an obstetrician to help her through her pregnancy with her son Bruno, she consulted many moms for referrals. She ended up choosing a woman her friend had recommended in part because of an extraordinary story the friend had told her about her obstetrician. During the massive blackout of 2003 that knocked out electricity in huge swaths of the Northeastern and Midwestern U.S., a patient of the obstetrician's went into labor. The two women were separated by nearly the entire length of the island of Manhattan. Due to the power outage, the subway system was down and the chance of hailing a cab was close to nil. Undeterred, the obstetrician leaped on her bicycle and rode all the way alongside the Westside Highway—and made it to her patient's bedside, with time to spare.

Lisa W. had heard many positive testimonials about other obstetricians' professionalism and commitment to their patients. But what stuck, what won her over and clinched the deal, was the image of this woman pumping furiously on the pedals of her bicycle on the side of the highway. The story was memorable because the friend who told it had included tangible, hard-to-forget details. These details add credibility to a story or claim and function like spiked crampons, digging into our memory.

Peter Jackson's 2005 remake of *King Kong* gave rise to an urban col-
loquialism, "Where's the monkey?"—a retort to Jackson's long-winded
build up to our first glimpse of the giant ape. The term translates roughly
to, "Will you cut to the chase already?"

Jackson's cinematic pacing aside, the point we want to make here
is that sometimes it's worth delaying the monkey by setting up the story
with vivid details and dramatic elements that ground your audience in
a time and place. When the monkey finally makes its appearance, the
result can be much more powerful and memorable.

Nonprofit Case Study: **Telling Margie's Story**

In 2004, Fenton had the privilege of publicizing the Goldman Environmental Prize, awarded each year by the San Francisco-based Goldman Fund to
grassroots environmental activists around the world. Margie Richard, 62, of
Louisiana, was among that year's winners, and the first African American to
receive the prize. As part of the press packet, Fenton drafted a winner profile
to stimulate news coverage.

Margie Richard was a middle school teacher turned environmental activist when she took it upon herself to hold Shell Chemicals accountable for
the devastating health problems in her hometown, caused by a neighboring
Shell plant and oil refinery.

We described the plant this way to provide a sense of scale—and
menace:

*Over the years, the plant, with its looming tanks and belching vapor
stacks, had grown to the size of nine football fields.*

And told the dramatic tale of how activists are made, not born:

*The defining event in her decision to become an activist occurred in 1973
when a Shell pipeline exploded, knocking one house off its foundation and
killing an elderly woman and a teenage boy who was mowing the lawn.
Richard recalls dashing out of her mother's house one block away and
spotting a body lying beneath a sheet and the 16-year-old boy, then still
alive, covered with raw burns. In 1988 another major industrial accident
killed seven workers and released 159 million pounds of toxins into the air.
Richard got in the habit of sleeping in her clothes so she could be ready to
jump out of bed and run for her life if needed.*

These details helped paint a picture for news producers and reporters, who
responded with extensive coverage, including a national ABC News "Person
of the Week" profile.

5. Appeal to group affiliations.

When we think about what motivates people to act on behalf of good causes, we sometimes trap ourselves in two camps. In one camp are the die-hards who are incredulous that people don't take action when the sky is clearly falling around them. In the other camp are the skeptics who believe people are strictly motivated by self-interest, willing to act only if they can see what's in it for them.

The problem with these camps is that they ignore another very important social influencer: an individual's self-identification as a member of a group. These groups can be your religion, your ethnicity, your sexual orientation, your political party, or your profession, whether you're a nurse or bike messenger.

In their book, *Made to Stick: Why Some Ideas Survive and Others Die,* Dan and Chip Heath describe a fascinating 1998 study that explores the relationship between political views and self-interest. Drawing from 30 years of research, Donald Kinder, a political science professor at the University of Michigan, turned conventional wisdom on its head by concluding that, when it comes to staking a political position, for the majority of people most of the time, self-interest takes a back seat to group interest.

Whether the topic is affirmative action or healthcare, people are less likely to cite personal benefits as influencing their thinking and more likely to weigh their decisions along value lines that they associate with protecting the greater good of the group. So, for example, an ethnic minority will support free speech, even if they are personally offended by racial slurs, or a single woman voter will support funding for schools even though she doesn't have children.

These findings are especially resonant for marketing to women because of women's strong affinity for "tribal" connections. A woman wants to feel part of a community, which means she is more inclined to factor into her decision making how her choices will reflect upon her position in the group and impact the group as a whole. This thinking process puts women in a third camp of decision making, one based on identity. In this model, the individual is more concerned with conforming to social norms and principles that help her answer the questions, "Who am I?" and "What would someone like me do?"

Below are two examples of how nonprofit groups have leveraged group affinity for good causes:

Nonprofit Case Study: **Happy Father's Day!
(Now Get Your Prostate Checked)**

Prostate cancer strikes one in six men. To make it worse, many men drag their feet, if they move their feet at all, when it comes to getting exams that could catch the disease early.

To help address the problem, Prostate Cancer Foundation launched a campaign on Father's Day in 2006 anchored by a national survey that found nearly three-quarters of men said they would be very likely to talk to their doctors about prostate cancer *if* the women in their lives prodded them to do so. So instead of targeting men directly, the foundation targeted the wives, daughters, and partners in men's lives by encouraging them to use Father's Day as a catalyst for introducing the topic, and to show they care.

Nonprofit Case Study: **What Would Jesus Drive?**

In 2002 a group called the Evangelical Environmental Network led by the Rev. Jim Ball launched a campaign called "What Would Jesus Drive?" It helped break the issue of fuel-efficiency from the exclusive realm of environmentalists into the much larger realm of the Christian faithful. Fuel-efficiency isn't just about vehicles, Rev. Ball argued. It's about values and being good stewards of the earth in our covenant with God.

The effort, driven by ads on CNN and on Christian radio, as well as a press conference featuring a convoy of nuns in hybrid cars, was designed to pressure the Big Three automakers in Detroit into building cleaner cars. It also generated more than 2,000 news stories worldwide and helped jumpstart a faith-based movement in pulpits across America to stop global warming. Years after "What Would Jesus Drive?" made headlines, its influence continues to be felt, with the public support in 2006 of 86 evangelical leaders (including the presidents of evangelical colleges, the head of Focus on the Family, and Rick Warren, mega-church pastor and author of the bestselling *The Purpose-Driven Life*) for federal legislation to reduce carbon dioxide emissions.

6. Tickle her funny bone.

Social change is serious work because the injustices we're struggling to right are no laughing matter. Little wonder that most nonprofits don't intuitively think to use humor in their communications. For some issues, humor won't work, period.

But for other issues, a flash of humor may be just the right thing. The social change field can feel oversaturated with images and messages

Storytelling through Video in the Age of YouTube

Advancements in video film and editing technology have made video production easier and more affordable. In turn, this has helped trigger the explosion of video posting and sharing online through Web sites like You-Tube. Increasingly, nonprofit organizations are getting into the game, featuring videos related to their work on their own Web sites. As a tool for storytelling, there is arguably no medium more powerful than the moving image, especially for bringing your issues to life in an immediate, visceral way.

As this book goes to print, more men than women watch online videos, but this gender split is expected to even out as younger generations raised on YouTube come of age. We delve deeper into online video consumption habits in Chapter 8, which examines how and where women get their news and information.

Here are five tips for effective online videos to promote social causes:

1. Keep it short: most people watch online videos at their desk during the flow of their workday and have time to view a one- to two-minute short.

2. Keep it moving: change up your settings and use voice-over and music to help thread your narrative because no one wants to watch a bunch of talking heads.

3. Quality counts: a professional-looking product is important for credibility, which is why talent counts both behind and in front of the camera.

4. Feature the people you help: think of these videos as opportunities for your supporters to meet the individuals whose lives they're working to improve.

5. Don't forget the "call to action" piece: whether it's integrated in the content or featured as a last screen, make sure you flash your URL and make an open invitation for people to get involved.

of suffering, deprivation, and doom. Humor can help your issue rise to the top by being memorable and unexpected.

Humor is also highly "viral." Think about the YouTube videos you've been forwarded or read about. Chances are high they were funny. Indeed, the defining video that arguably helped catapult YouTube into the mainstream was the wildly popular *Saturday Night Live* skit, "Lazy Sunday Afternoon," about two New York City slackers preparing to see *The Chronicles of Narnia*.

Now here's the catch. If women are your target audience, what makes them laugh?

This question has been a source of some long-standing controversy. In the January 2007 issue of *Vanity Fair* titled, "Why Women Aren't Funny," Christopher Hitchens tries on various theories, from *men will laugh at anything because they're more stupid* to *women are more serious because childbirth is no joke.* Then he hits on this observation: "Male humor prefers the laugh at someone's expense, and understands that life is quite possibly a joke to begin with," whereas, "women, bless their tender hearts, would prefer that life be fair, and even sweet, rather than the sordid mess it really is."

Hitchens is right on his first point, at least according to experts who have studied the subject and concluded that men's humor often stems from being "on top" and feeling superior, usually at someone else's expense.

Take the long-running (and award-winning) radio ad series for Bud Light, "Real Men of Genius." Each episode pays mock tribute to an "unsung hero" in American culture, from "Mr. Really Bad Toupee Wearer" to "Mr. Fancy Coffee Shop Coffee Pourer" and "Mr. Really Loud Cell Phone Talker Guy." Even the ads that appear to be delivering genuine praise do so in a somewhat superior and knowing tone. The audience here is definitely men.

Women, on the other hand, because of their highly attuned radar for empathy, are less likely to find this brand of one-upmanship funny. This is where Hitchens takes a wrong turn: It's not that women aren't funny. It's that their funny bones are different from men's.

Women are less likely to laugh *at* someone than at a situation, particularly if it's a situation with which they can identify.

Don't get us wrong. There are plenty of women who love *South Park* and *Family Guy*. But you're more likely to score points with a marketing campaign that's less about snark and more about triggering a grin of recognition. Below is an example of a nonprofit online campaign that used humor to generate fundraising dollars.

Nonprofit Case Study: **CODEPINK**

If you've read this far, then you know we're not fans of "pink-washing"—marketing campaigns that window-dress products or causes in pink to reach women, but with nothing *there* once you peel back the curtain.

CODEPINK is one organization that turns pink on its head. Launched in 2002 by activists Medea Benjamin, Jodie Evans, and Gael Murphy, CODE-PINK first made headlines when members began holding vigils in front of the White House and outside President Bush's Crawford, Texas ranch to pro-test the War in Iraq. Since then, CODEPINK groups have sprung up in more than 250 communities in the U.S. and abroad.

Whether they're crashing the Democratic and Republican conventions or lobbying policymakers to bring the troops home, the group brings its unique brand of sly political humor to a dead-serious topic. They've handed out "pink slips" to war makers and supporters at Halliburton shareholder meetings and big-money political fundraisers. On their award-winning Web site, you can buy pink T-shirts emblazoned with slogans including, "Mother with a Cause," "Give Peace a Vote," and "Gandhi is My Homeboy."

We asked Medea Benjamin to reflect on humor as a force for change:

How did you come up with the concept and name for "CODEPINK"?

Medea: "We chose pink to respond to the Bush Administration's color-coded alerts—yellow, orange, red. We wanted hot pink, but the URL was a porn site. So we settled with pink. The response has been very funny. Some women (and men) embrace it and go nuts—pink boas, boots, and panties. Others, who love CODEPINK but hate pink, wear it sparingly, and even grudg-ingly. There's a cute song someone just wrote for us about the color. I love the second verse, which says, 'Mama take a good look now, your baby's wearing pink' because I know so many young women who wear strictly black, and are very serious about their politics. Their mothers now marvel to see them in pink!" *CODEPINK pulls no punches, but it's also known for its sense of humor. Can you say more about why humor can be an effective force for activism and organizing?*

Medea: "Humor is the leaven that keeps us buoyed despite the grim reality of war. Humor allows us to keep pressuring Congress, day after day, with no obvious results. Humor keeps our community together and keeps us from taking ourselves too seriously. And humor allows us to attract attention when the media yawns at traditional protests. It's a great antidote to the high and mighty."

Conclusion

It may be stating the obvious to say we want our audiences to care about the issues. But sometimes we get so wrapped up in the work that we forget to back up and frame things in ways that will stop people in their tracks, tug their heartstrings, and pull them in. The strategies we dis-cussed in this chapter, including telling stories and appealing to people's group identification, work for both women *and* men (who doesn't love a good story?), but they are especially useful for getting your issue onto women's radar. These "Care" strategies are more essential than ever in today's information-saturated culture—where the average American is exposed to anywhere from 600 to 3,000 advertisements a day. Each of the strategies is basically a way to help you stand out from the data glut, and to sidestep two pitfalls of poor communications: tired, yawn-inducing abstractions and the eyes-glazing-over effect of rolling out facts at the expense of making an emotional appeal.

Now that you've got your audience's heart in your hands (and top of mind), we'll move onto the "Connect" principle, another powerful force for attracting women's support and for creating the kind of social transformation we want to see in the world.

Chapter Take-Aways

Put the principle of care at the center of your marketing efforts to women with the following tips:

- Put a face on your organization.

- Keep it simple—and real.

- Tell real-life stories.

- Don't leave out details.

- Appeal to people's sense of group affiliation.

- Use humor.

5

Connect

Making the Connection

In previous chapters we've described how women value community and connecting with others, as a survival mechanism, and as a way of life. In place of competition and one-upmanship, they see cooperation and strong social relationships as the solution to many of life's—and the world's—problems. And, as we'll show, women aren't the only ones who crave community.

In this chapter, we apply these principles to the realm of communications and marketing by showing how the power of connecting can contribute to your ability to attract and retain loyal supporters to your cause, campaign, and organization. When you look for, and act on, opportunities that help women connect, you are creating opportunities to trigger fundraising and activism. When we talk about connecting, there are three areas where the principle applies:

1. Connect people with your organization through community.

2. Connect through creativity.

3. Connect women with each other.

1. Connect people to your organization through community.

In his influential book, *Bowling Alone: The Collapse and Revival of American Community*, Robert D. Putnam describes the decline of social capital and civic engagement as more and more Americans find themselves disconnected from family, friends, neighbors, and a broader sense of community. We are increasingly watching Netflix movies at home alone instead of going to the movie theater. We listen to our iPods on the subway and as we walk down the street. We buy books and CDs online instead of browsing in stores. Families seldom eat dinner together anymore. Our technology has made personal choice and our lives more efficient, but it has also set a pace and created a way of life that increasingly makes social bonds and human connection more tenuous.

Savvy corporate marketing executives have tapped into the anxiety and yearning for more social connection that has grown out of these alienating trends by developing advertising campaigns that showcase their products as catalysts for social glue in consumers' lives—especially the lives of women. When you supply this social glue, you connect people to the positive associations they will have with your brand and product.

Those of us who are in the social change business recognize that our work can often feel like a Sisyphean struggle against forces often much larger, better funded, and more powerful than our own. A great deal of our "job satisfaction," if you will, comes from working in the trenches with like-minded people, whether they are our co-workers or the broad community of activists and supporters who join us in our struggles. Little wonder that one of the most beloved quotations for the nonprofit sector (and one that often appears as the tagline to email signatures) is anthropologist Margaret Mead's observation, "Never doubt that a small group of thoughtful, committed citizens can change the world. Indeed, it is the only thing that ever has."

In other words, a strong sense of community is naturally built into our work, but many of us don't make as much active use of this emotional phenomenon as we could.

But enough "tell." Here are a few examples from both the business and nonprofit sectors to show you what we mean:

Corporate Case Study: **Beyond Snap, Crackle, and Pop: "Childhood is Calling"**

The current advertising campaign for Kellogg's Rice Krispies depicts a mother bonding with her children in the kitchen as they make Rice Krispies treats. Snap, Crackle, and Pop have been replaced by a deep adult nostalgia about making marshmallow snacks with our own parents: "Spending time in the kitchen with your kids is a great way to make lasting memories."

Click on their Web site, www.childhoodiscalling.com, and you'll find more easy-to-make recipes you can prepare with your kids as well as safety tips for children in the kitchen. There's even a pull down menu so you can show your children what the cereal box design looked like back when you were a kid. The marketing strategy is less about the cereal itself as it is about what role the cereal has played in our family lives and the happy memories it evokes.

Corporate Case Study: **A Smart Approach to Marketing Cell Phone Plans—"Fave Five"**

Some cell phone companies have taken this "connector" strategy to heart. Rather than boast about the number of free minutes, the reliability of the reception, or their high-tech features, T-Mobile has centered its marketing campaign, "Stick Together," on how their service can help their customers stay in touch with the people they care about. T-Mobile figured out that most people make at least two-thirds of their calls to the same five phone numbers every month—hence the phone company's "Fave Five" plan, which offers unlimited calls to the five numbers you call most. T-Mobile also recognized, of course, that moms are making the decision about which cell phone plan to purchase for their families.

Nonprofit Case Study: **MoveOn.org —Party For the Planet**

MoveOn.org is often credited for helping to pioneer a successful model for online political organizing. While the Internet was certainly essential to the group's success, MoveOn.org also deserves credit for building and sustaining a progressive community that extends beyond its virtual roots, bringing people together face-to-face for a common cause.

MoveOn.org has encouraged their members to hold bake sales in their neighborhoods to raise money for causes and candidates. They've used Web 2.0 technology to enable people across the country to open their homes for "house parties" to screen documentary films about the Iraq War and Fox News' right-wing bias. They've held ice cream socials that doubled as "get out the vote" campaigns where members, armed with their cell phones, gathered in homes and community centers to call registered voters to hit the polls.

On a hot July evening in New York's Lower East Side, a group of about ten people, including a music director for a smooth jazz station, a student in illustration design, and a PhD in physics, gathered in the kitchen of a walk-up tenement apartment. Most of them were strangers to each other, but they were there for "Party for the Planet," one of hundreds of similar events organized online around the country by MoveOn.org members. Billed as "the biggest party the planet has ever needed," the informal potlucks brought together thousands of people to watch the Live Earth concerts and taped interviews of presidential candidates who had agreed to answer a handful of questions on climate change from MoveOn.org members.

Over Japanese cold noodles, Anja Olbrisch, the host of the Lower East Side event with her partner, Tetsu Ohara, explained how she first learned about MoveOn.org during one of a series of protests the group organized in the lead up to the Iraq War. She remembers trudging through Central Park in the dead of winter to attend one such protest and being both surprised and elated to discover 8,000 other people who had braved the weather to stand in solidarity for a cause they believed in.

"There are so few [political] events locally," said Olbrisch, an art director for an advertising firm. "What I like about MoveOn events is that the same kind of people show up. Good friendships have grown out of these events."

Jen Senko, a documentary film producer and a desk-top publishing consultant at the gathering, remembers feeling "alone and angry" about the political direction the country was going. Joining MoveOn gave her ballast.

"It was really wonderful to hook up with a community that was like-minded," Senko said. "You really feel it's like a community. I don't want to just complain. I'm interested in fighting!"

The Aspiration for Community

In raising the "Bowling Alone" theory, we don't mean to overstate our case. Americans may be living a more isolated existence compared to previous generations, but we are social creatures at heart, which means regardless of the ebb and flow of social trends, connection with other people will always have its appeal.

In a marketplace where, for every product or service there are dozens of companies offering virtually the same thing (the nonprofit sector is no exception), you can give yourself an added advantage by creating a space for your brand that fulfills people's aspiration for community.

2. Connect through creativity.

In 2006, *Time* magazine made the unconventional decision to name "You" as its Person of the Year. Their reasoning? The big story that year was about "community and collaboration on a scale never seen before," driven by the emergence of digital democracy innovations like Wikipedia, YouTube, and MySpace, and wildly popular programs like *American Idol* that invited viewers to pick their favorites and determine the outcome of the show.

Online companies also got into the act. Netflix, the online movie rental service, for example, offers a feature called "Movie Sliders" that allows you to see what your friends are watching and how they rate movies they've seen. Amazon.com also offers interactive, information sharing features like consumer reviews and "wish lists" where others can see books and other items you'd welcome as gifts in your mailbox.

This democratizing trend, realized with the help of new media technology, is also creating exciting opportunities for forward-looking nonprofits to connect with members, donors, and activists as never before. These innovations are an opportunity and a challenge for the nonprofit sector to go beyond its traditional "Get Involved" comfort zone, which typically involves inviting people to either make a donation or send a letter to an elected official. But "getting involved" today can mean much more if you're willing to make the investment. Offering a two-way street that solicits the creativity and opinions of new and existing supporters can help you build loyalty and a more invested constituency base. It's also the direction that Web 2.0 technology is driving communications today.

For nonprofits, this type of creative and democratic participation can take many forms. Perhaps one of the most high-profile examples in recent years was MoveOn.org's 2004 "Bush in 30 Seconds" contest.

Nonprofit Case Study: **"Bush in 30 Seconds"**
The brainchild of MoveOn Cultural Director Laura Dawn, techno artist Moby, and MoveOn Executive Director Eli Pariser, the contest was an open invitation to produce a 30-second video spot critical of President George W. Bush that MoveOn.org vowed to air during the Super Bowl XXXVIII broadcast, typically the most-watched television event of the year.

More than 1,500 people produced and submitted entries. About 100,000 people voted for their favorites online, winnowing the pool to a list of finalists that were then judged by a panel of celebrities and media experts. The winning spot, created by a Charlie Fisher of Denver, Colorado, depicts a dystopian vision of the future in which children are indentured as dishwashers, janitors, and assembly line workers to pay off President Bush's $1 trillion deficit.

The contest itself became a cause célèbre in the media. Coverage only intensified when CBS rejected the winning ad for being too "controversial" for broadcast. The ad eventually aired elsewhere, including CNN during Super Bowl halftime and on the same day as Bush's State of the Union address. By then the exposure online and in the news media had created a maelstrom of publicity for MoveOn.org's referendum on Bush. The contest also had the effect of opening up the specialized world of political TV advertising—formerly the bastion of highly paid consultants—to anyone with a good concept and a working knowledge of do-it-yourself video technology.

Below we describe another example of collaborative activism in action—this time from the labor movement.

Nonprofit Case Study: **Since Sliced Bread**
—Citizen Solutions to the Healthcare Crisis
One of the most exciting and energized developments in the labor movement today is the Service Employees International Union (SEIU). The union represents 1.8 million mostly low-wage workers—janitors and nurses and home health care aides—many of whom have never belonged to a union.

Today the SEIU is the largest and fastest-growing union in the country, thanks in no small part to its president, Andy Stern, who has tapped into a large vein of popular unrest about today's cut-throat global economy (particularly the bottom-line business practices of mega-corporations like Wal-Mart) that is squeezing out the nation's middle class and driving American jobs overseas.

To grow support for union workers and, more broadly, for America's working class, Stern helped found PurpleOcean.org in 2004, a political network and affiliate group of more than 100,000 Americans who don't belong to unions, but who share the SEIU's interest in winning better wages and health care for workers nationwide.

"We know that even if we build strength in our industries, no one union, including SEIU, can succeed as an isolated island of strength in a non-union sea," Stern said in a recent convention speech. "As the largest union, it is our job to help rebuild U.S. labor's strength."

Like MoveOn.org, PurpleOcean.org fights for change through online campaigns. Gina Glantz, the senior adviser on the project, hired the gurus responsible for orchestrating Howard Dean's groundbreaking Internet-driven political campaign to help create PurpleOcean.org, whose activities have included:

- **Since Sliced Bread**—An online contest, with a $100,000 prize, that invited people to submit their best new economic idea for helping working families. In addition to the prize money, SEIU committed to work to make the idea a reality. The contest winner, a 41-year-old project manager from Seattle, Wash., proposed imposing a "resource tax" on pollution and fossil fuels, that would fund renewable-energy research and environmental restoration.

- **Wal-Mart Fact Checker**—A "spread the word" contest that offered to pay $1,000 toward the winner's health insurance premiums if he or she were one of the first 25 participants to get 200 people to sign up via email to learn more about the campaign targeting Wal-Mart's shoddy labor practices. And if the winner already had employer-paid health insurance, the prize could be transferred to a Wal-Mart employee without health benefits. PurpleOcean.org also made a point of soliciting members for their feedback and opinions on how to best advance the campaign.

A Win-Win Collaboration

In both these campaigns, ordinary citizens were invited to "own" the cause. PurpleOcean.org was clever with its use of incentives to stimulate the public's creativity and form ties based on a shared commitment to economic justice. These ties are leveraged by the SEIU for organizing purposes, helping to turn out the famed "purple army" of supporters at public actions to push for workers' rights.

The benefits to this approach are multiple. Nonprofits get to tap into a pool of ingenuity and talent. Supporters get a chance to contribute to their favorite nonprofit and cause in a more direct and fun way. Such campaigns get a boost of energy and exposure they would not otherwise receive, in part by involving supporters on the ground floor of their conception. And when all is said and done, these efforts will have strengthened the bond between the sponsoring nonprofit and its supporters because it gives supporters more ownership of the project. It also gives the nonprofit a platform to engage its community of supporters beyond asking them to cut a check.

3. Connect women with each other.

As we've shown, community-building matters to both men and women, but for women, bonding with their female friends holds a special place in their hearts. This is especially true as women get older. Since Lisa C.'s mom retired, for example, she spends more of her time playing bridge and hiking with her girlfriends. Last year she took her first cruise with friends she made as a junior high school student in Taiwan. These girlfriends connect her with her past, and help her make sense of her present as they go through many of the same life changes as professionals, mothers, and, for some of them, grandmothers.

The extraordinary value that women place on their relationships with other women has a direct bearing on how they want to be marketed to. A study by Grey Advertising found that 74 percent of women would like to see advertising that shows more women doing things together with their girlfriends, sisters, and moms.

When you connect women to each other, you strengthen your brand. This is because, as we've noted earlier, women are twice as likely as male customers to make referrals. So, if you reach one woman, she'll spread the word. But if you put two women together, your word-of-mouth potential grows exponentially.

Entire commercial industries have capitalized on this very phenomenon (think Avon and Tupperware) but recent years have seen a proliferation of marketing campaigns that tap into female bonding, even for products that are not typically associated with exclusively women-centered products. Proctor and Gamble, for example, recently launched a series of online forums on topics that women are typically passionate about, such as breast cancer and careers, and invited women to offer their opinions and post personal stories. Proctor and Gamble used the forums to help them gain greater insight into their customers' wants and needs. Here's another recent corporate example:

Corporate Case Study: **"Play Date"**

A recent TV ad for Tostitos features three women, all mothers, laughing and chatting on the couch, munching on chips and salsa. One of the moms leans over and says, "We ought to do play dates more often." Another mom nods in agreement, "I think the kids really enjoy it."

The camera cuts to a shot of three tiny babies tucked tightly in their carry strollers, arranged side by side on the floor and completely oblivious to one other. The women burst into laughter as the voiceover says, "Make any get together better. Good things happen at the Tostitos."

In this commercial, the chips themselves are there to serve a much more powerful and winning concept: women enjoying each other's company.

Women aren't the only ones who want to bond with friends, of course, as countless male-bonding beer commercials will attest to. Other commercials in the Tostitos ad series show an entire family bonding over chips, from teenagers to grandparents. What the Tostitos ad about the moms illustrates, however, is marketing savvy about who holds the purse strings on general consumer goods.

Nonprofits would do well to try similar tactics that bring women together, particularly for fundraising purposes. Below we describe two such fundraising efforts that do double duty as awareness-building campaigns.

Nonprofit Case Study: **The Women's Funding Network and Lifetime Take on Human Trafficking**

In October 2005 Lifetime Television premiered a two-part miniseries, *Human Trafficking*, starring Academy Award winner Mira Sorvino as a federal agent hot on the trail of a Russian sex trafficking ring. The Women's Funding Network (WFN), an international network of women's and girls' funds, partnered with Lifetime to leverage the miniseries as a tool to educate and drive action on behalf of the 800,000 people, most of them women, who fall victim to the multibillion-dollar modern slavery racket.

Using online social networking technology, WFN encouraged its members and women across the globe to host house parties for other women on the two nights the TV movie aired. In total, 73 women offered to hold events across 28 states, from Hawaii to Pennsylvania. House parties also took place in other countries.

Hosts downloaded an online toolkit that included a discussion guide and tips on event logistics. Also looped into the campaign was an advocacy component: Participants were asked to sign a petition urging U.S. Representatives to pass a bill that would protect women from unscrupulous international marriage brokers. The campaign exceeded its goal of collecting 15,000 signatures by amassing 18,128 signatures. For the Women's Funding Network, it was also an opportunity to brand their organization and build out their Rolodex of women around the country committed to advancing women's issues.

"What this campaign demonstrated to our community of women's funds from around the world is that women are not only relational in their giving, but also in their activism. When women think about either giving or doing for the sake of making their communities safer and healthier, they look for other groupings of women who share similar values and visions for the future," stated Chris Grumm, president and CEO of the Women's Funding Network. "This is the premise upon which women's funds from around the world are based and has proven an effective strategy in the building of these funds who have given away over $400 million in the past 20 years to improve the lives of women and their families."

Nonprofit Case Study: **Women for Women International —Breaking Down Borders**

Zainab Salbi was inspired to found Women for Women International in 1993 after reading a harrowing story in a magazine about rape camps in Bosnia and Herzegovina. From the beginning, one of the driving engines of her organization has been its "sister" sponsorship program, which matches American donors with women in war-torn regions, from Afghanistan to Sudan, working to rebuild their lives and communities.

In just 14 years, the program's 125,000 donors, each giving monthly donations of $27, have helped raise more than $39 million to seed small businesses and pay for job-skills training, education, and other essentials for women working to get their families on the path to financial security.

"The sponsorship program simply recognized the power of the individual," said Salbi. "In a world that is characterized by so many wars and conflicts, we often talk about the military solutions. What is not talked about as often is how women are taking ownership of their own resources and voices and reaching out to their sisters whose lives have been destroyed by war. The most solid way to build peace is through the creation of jobs, through ensuring every child goes to school, through respecting the dignity of each individual, and through sharing our love with each other."

Within the connection developed when one woman helps another woman, lies the power to make a difference—individually and as a worldwide community of women.

Two Mothers, A World Apart: **Liz and Violette's Story**

When Liz Hammer, a mother of two in Boston, signed up with Women for Women International's sponsorship program, she was matched with Violette Mutegwamaso, herself a mother of a boy and girl in Rwanda.

Violette's life was turned upside down in 1994 when civil war broke out between the Hutu and Tutsi. When violence threatened to erupt in her small village, she was forced to flee with her two children to a nearby church. But instead of providing sanctuary, the church was attacked by machete-wielding militia. By pretending to be dead, Violette and her children managed to be among a handful of survivors of a massacre that claimed 700 lives.

Violette found herself struggling to support her family on meager earnings from farming other people's land, but it was not enough. Medicine, clothes, and schooling were out of the question.

With support from Liz, however, Violette was able to invest in a fledgling business harvesting sorghum and brewing the grain into drink. The two women began exchanging letters. Violette reported on the growth of her business, which expanded to buying sorghum from other local farmers and growing beans that she used to both feed her family and sell for profit. Soon she was hiring other women in the community to work the fields. She applied for a bank loan to route a water pipe into her village so women would not have to walk for hours with heavy jugs to reach a water tap.

Of Violette, Liz has said, "I think about her all the time, in fact, on a daily basis. I just had my second girl, and between her and my two-year-old toddler, it just seems like a lot. I sometimes feel overwhelmed and there is too much to handle. But then I think of Violette, and women like her. What I have gone through is so little in comparison to her. She has provided me with tremendous perspective that you can't get from just reading an article or reading a news story."

In November 2007 Women for Women surprised a room full of supporters at their annual gala by finally uniting Liz and Violette. The room was full of applause, tears, and netted more than 465 new sponsors.

Nonprofit Case Study: **Supporting the Troops at Home**

You don't have to be a big organization with millions (or even hundreds) of members in order to put the "Connecting" principle into action. Recently, Fenton worked with Microsoft and United Service Organization (USO)—the group best known for sending Bob Hope and other entertainers to support the troops abroad—on a campaign to honor everyday volunteers who support the troops and veterans at home.

The centerpiece of the campaign was a citizens' award contest, with nominees selected from around the country. The final winners included some amazing women and men who literally ran their operations from their living rooms, yet had managed to grow impressive networks of volunteers united by a shared mission. Among them: Socks for Soldiers, Inc., an organization started by Kim Opperman of Shelby, Ohio, that has grown from a one-woman operation into a network of 1,500 volunteers who are hand-knitting military regulation socks for the troops abroad. The idea began when Kim, a single mother of six, knitted a pair for her own son, who is serving with the Air Force overseas. It got her thinking. What if she could knit 100,000 socks for soldiers stationed abroad?

Volunteers from around the world have since taken on her "20 minutes a day—one pair of socks" challenge. Before they are mailed off, the socks are stuffed with toiletries like lip balm and toothbrushes. Kim continues to run the operation from her living room. She calls her computer keyboard "command central."

Conclusion

Nearly every nonprofit we've worked with has told us they want to cultivate a larger and more active membership. Doing so, however, may require rethinking business as usual. If you invite supporters to "Get Involved" and limit their options to writing a check or signing up for a newsletter, you aren't fully taking advantage of people's creativity and energy. You also aren't speaking to their desire to belong to a grassroots community of like-minded change agents. Innovative public sector leaders have found that when they create opportunities for people to collaborate with others and bring more of themselves into their activism, the results are much more powerful. Sometimes connecting people to your issue means connecting them with each other.

In the next few pages, we'll confront the "tough customer" challenge as it refers to attracting women's support and why it's worth the effort (hint: the "Connecting" principle plays a big role). The chapter will end by focusing on an innovative, grassroots fundraising strategy driven by women that may point to the future of philanthropy and political giving.

Chapter Take-Aways

- Women value community and connection. When you identify and put forward opportunities that help women connect, you are creating opportunities to trigger fundraising and activism. You can do this by:

    —connecting people with your organization through community;

    —connecting people by harnessing their collective creativity; and

    —connecting women with each other.

When you connect women to each other, you strengthen your brand.

6

Cultivate

Tell Me More

When marketing consultant Wendy Dembo was stopped in front of her local Whole Food supermarket by a volunteer seeking donations for Save the Children, she took the opportunity to ask the volunteer a series of questions about what the organization did, where her money would go, and specifically how much of it would go directly to children in need.

Wendy wasn't purposefully trying to give the solicitor a hard time. She was just doing what came naturally to her—and to many women—when confronted with the opportunity to either purchase something or donate to a good cause.

"I am not a compulsive shopper, so I think twice about making purchases. And that goes for donating to charities as well. I want to know the facts, how much money goes to administration and how much goes towards helping people, animals, or the environment. And I am sure that there are other women who want to make sure that their money is really going to a good cause and not to fancy lunches." Wendy said.

Remember our frustrated political fundraising friend who had thrown up her hands at trying to solicit donations from women? The same challenge applies: women take longer to cultivate than men because they're more likely to demand more information before they're willing to say "yes."

Given the resource investment required to solicit women's support, it is unsurprising that women made just 27 percent of all donations to political candidates in the 2006 elections, according to a study by Women's Campaign Forum Foundation of trends in women's political giving. (It's important to note that the Federal Election Commission only reports individual donations at or exceeding $200.) In the case of single and combined gifts over $1,000, women accounted for 28 percent of donations—a percentage that has not changed in a decade.

By the simplest cost-labor analysis, you'd think cultivating women's support wouldn't be worth the time or effort. In fact, the opposite is true.

Changing Trends in Philanthropy

One of the hottest trends in philanthropy right now, and one that appears to be here to stay, is the greater attention funders are paying to evaluating and measuring social change results. In other words, funders are becoming "tougher customers" too, by requiring nonprofits to do a better job of demonstrating return on investment and a sound and strategic approach to allocating resources. While the metrics for measuring the impact on society and the environment remains to some degree a work in progress, public interest organizations that are adept at connecting the dots between their work and real-world results will win funders' trust. In large, this means meeting high thresholds for information and transparency in how that information is available, which also happen to be touchstones for winning women's support.

Women are More Loyal and Often More Involved

Because women are tougher customers, the nonprofit or political campaign has to supply much more relevant, meaningful information to convince women that they've made the right choice. And while we know women may take longer to sign on the dotted line, the fact is, we also know that when they do, their loyalty and commitment is golden. Moreover, nonprofit funding experts have found that with men, signing the check is often the be-all, end-all of their support, whereas with women, the reverse is often true: giving money often represents just the surface of a deep well of support and involvement that nonprofits can draw from again and again.

Researchers have found that men (and here we are generalizing, of course) are more likely to give to a cause that will result in some type of personal recognition (such as a new medical facility) and that supports the status quo (such as alumni giving to a university), while women are more motivated to give to help others in need or achieve a measure of positive social change. This gender split represents a huge opportunity, particularly for nonprofits that are driven by a strong humanitarian or social change agenda. As we've discussed earlier, women's desire to *change* the status quo is believed to be a contributing factor in the soaring number of female donors in this year's presidential election.

Women = Word of Mouth

Anyone who has searched online for a hotel, restaurant, or any number of products or services knows that testimonials from ordinary consumers have become an ingrained part of the process. The public research firm RoperASW, which has tracked the influence of word-of-mouth referrals over the decades has found that, 20 years ago, 67 percent of Americans said word of mouth was an important source of information for their decision-making. By 1992, 92 percent said they relied on word of mouth as a key factor.

As we've described in earlier chapters, women are twice as likely as male customers to make referrals. According to Delia Passi, the former publisher of *Working Woman* magazine, and the co-author of *Winning the Toughest Customer: The Essential Guide to Selling to Women*, "When you create and sustain a relationship with a female customer, you set up a system that will pay off in multiples down the road. They'll stick with you, and they'll build your pipeline of referrals by spreading the word."

Fast-Forwarded Election Cycle

One of the most striking developments in the 2008 elections was how early presidential hopefuls began "exploring" their candidacies and throwing their hat in the ring compared to years previous. The starting gate opens much sooner now. This longer election cycle means that candidates and their campaign staff now have more time to win women's support, which as a general rule, requires more time to cultivate. In 2006, if women had increased their giving by 22 percent, it would have represented an additional $43 million for candidates.

Six Keys to Cultivating Women's Support

Great, you're thinking. I want a piece of that action. So what does it take to bring women under your tent? The short answer is by offering as much transparency as possible about the impact of your work and where their investment goes. The same "tough customer" principle behind why women consumers generally take longer to shop for products holds true when they go about selecting a cause to support.

We offer six concrete strategies for cultivating women's support:

1. Think long-term.

2. Don't just ask for money.

3. Show where the money goes.

4. Leverage third-party validators.

5. Demonstrate your impact.

6. Make her feel part of a group effort.

1. Think long-term.

The first rule of cultivating women donors is to think long-term. As we've described in this chapter and elsewhere, women take longer to make up their minds about whether to support an organization. They are more likely than men to involve others in their decision-making process and to run through a check-list of criteria before they are fully assured that their decision is the best one.

The pay-off is worth it. This is true even from a pure numbers perspective: women tend to live longer than men, which means it is they who will hold the keys to much of the $41 to $136 trillion that is expected to transfer from generation to generation over the next 50 years.

Development officers at some nonprofits already take these points to heart as part of their efforts to cultivate "legacy" giving, or donations through individuals' wills and trusts. They understand, however, that this type of "ask" can't come from out of left field; instead, it is best grown out of a long-standing relationship with a donor who has come to know the organization well and holds its mission close to his or her heart.

2. Don't just ask for money.

So what does long-term cultivation look like? For starters, it may not mean that money is the first or only thing you ask for. Remember that women are voracious information-seekers and that they're also more likely than men to want to build a relationship with the organization they support. This means creating educational opportunities for them to get to know your group better, including opportunities for volunteering with you, as fundraising experts have found that women are more likely to open their pocketbooks to an organization if they've volunteered there first. The strategies outlined below offer other specific ideas for providing opportunities that will help familiarize and connect women donors to your organization.

3. Show where the money goes.

Top of mind for many donors is the assurance that their money will go where they intend it to go. They want to see a straight pipeline between their donation and the program work or direct service that benefits the cause or target population they signed up to support. Red flags go up when an organization can't prove that most of their funding goes to these areas. Nothing rankles like finding out a nonprofit pours as much money into fundraising as into making the world a better place.

This requires providing a breakdown of your spending up front in your direct mail fundraising appeals, your Web site, and other communications vehicles. Many nonprofits provide this level of transparency, but they do so only in their annual report, which few people actually see. Treat your small donors as you would your major donors, because while the amount they give may differ, their concerns are the same. They want proof that their money is going to the right place.

Here's how one group, Save the Children, is connecting the dots for donors:

Nonprofit Case Study: **Save the Children**

As it turns out, Wendy needn't have worried about Save the Children, which was founded to help impoverished families in the Appalachians who were hit hard during the Great Depression. Since then, it has evolved into an international relief and development organization.

The organization is well aware of the importance of being up front about its money trail. Right on the home page of its Web site, Save the Children prominently features its financial information in a section titled, "How We Use Our Funds." Ninety percent of the donations it receives goes directly to communities in need, with program services like health aid for HIV/AIDS, education, and food security.

For would-be donors who require even greater assurance, Save the Children also posts its most recent financial statements, including excerpts from 990 forms, and acknowledges that operating revenues in 2005 were greater than those in 2006 because of the gifts received for the Asian tsunami crisis.

Where Are You on the Shelf?

The key to information-sharing is to anticipate and answer questions donors may not even know they have. This can help build their confidence in who you are and how you operate. When women do their homework, they may have a checklist, but they are also in exploratory mode: all their channels are open to absorbing a variety of inputs that will help them arrive at the Perfect Answer.

To the frustration of men who hate shopping but get dragged along for the ride, this "open channel" approach is how women often get things done. When Lisa C.'s sister went with her husband to IKEA recently, they had two totally different ideas about how to shop. Cynthia's husband wanted to make a bee-line for the items on their shopping list—in and out. But Cynthia insisted on strolling through the aisles. "How else am I supposed to get ideas?" she asked. If she hadn't made an exploratory run, she explained, she would never have stumbled across the white cotton seat cushions that now cover all her dining room chairs.

Like the science that goes into how supermarkets organize goods on their shelf space, IKEA was savvy about where to display those seat cushions, in the dining room furnishings department. Likewise, nonprofits should be thoughtful about where to display information—not buried in newsletters or annual reports that are likely to get archived (and where we as consultants often find the best stories buried), but right out front in the places where would-be donors are likely to click or flip through as they're learning about you and making their assessment about whether to support you.

Securing Core Support

You can't blame donors for wanting to see their money go directly to people in need. But we recognize that this puts undue pressure on nonprofits that also must cover operational expenses. Funding for these operational needs, also known as core support, is what keeps nonprofits running. It can mean everything from the big stuff—staff hires and pay increases and paying the rent to relatively small (but no less critical) maintenance needs, like upgrading a database or replacing a broken fax machine.

A number of foundations have responded by trying to influence the broader philanthropic community to value and give operating support. The Blue Shield of California Foundation, for example, makes general core support grants to domestic violence shelters, with the understanding that the money may be used to keep the lights on—literally—or improve their phone system, and to diabetes clinics that may use these flexible funds to cover patients who don't have health insurance and fall between the cracks of private and public aid.

Nonprofit organizations can also think outside the box by being transparent about their needs and how individual donors can help. While a majority of donors will remain primarily interested in supporting program services, a smaller group may be sympathetic and even enthusiastic about providing targeted support to appeals for a "rapid response fund" that will allow you to jump on a related news opportunity, or to be among a handful of donors who understands that the traditional sources of funding can leave critical gaps. Schools, for example, have had great success soliciting support from parents and local businesses to cover very specific expenses like books or sports equipment. This type of appeal to fulfill a highly specific need can also fulfill a donor's desire to direct money to something more targeted and concrete.

4. Leverage third-party validators.

The messenger can often be as important as the message when it comes to establishing your credibility. This is where testimonials from third parties—those people or organizations apart from your organization—come in handy. It's why Listerine constantly toots the fact that it is the "number one dentist-recommended brand of mouth rinse" and the only over-the-counter mouth rinse that carries a "Seal of Acceptance" from the American Dental Association. It's also why a recommendation from Oprah can sell millions of books—or drive down beef prices and get her in hot water with the cattle industry.

Marketing experts will tell you that female consumers especially have their ear open for testimonials from trusted sources. Women are more likely than men to involve others in their decision-making. Men are more prone to "go it alone" because they perceive advice-seeking as undermining their own decision-making authority. Women, on the other hand, have no inhibitions about consulting others. This doesn't mean they don't trust their own judgment. Rather, this outside input (particularly from someone with greater expertise) becomes another notch on their due-diligence belt.

Once women complete their homework and "sign up," so to speak, they are also more likely than men to be open to and rely on an organization's advice. After all, they've already made that organization jump through multiple hoops to win their trust, which makes their confidence and faith in the organization that much stronger.

In our line of work, we often advise our nonprofit clients to cultivate positive testimonials about their organization from respected stakeholders connected to their issues, whether it's an elected official, an expert in their field, or a community leader. These validating quotations can be used on their Web sites, in their brochures, and any number of marketing and fundraising tools. A quotation from an individual representative of the group's targeted population, whether it's a welfare-to-work mom or a victim of gun violence, can also be a powerful endorsement.

What follows is an example of how one nonprofit organization spotlights its "trusted advisors":

Nonprofit Case Study: **Room to Read**

Room to Read, which establishes schools and libraries in partnership with local communities in the developing world, was founded by former Microsoft executive John Wood, who took an unplanned detour that would change his life while on a backpacking vacation in the Himalayas. Wood encountered a small schoolhouse in Nepal that had hardly any books. The encounter so moved him that when he returned to the states, he collected 3,000 book donations from friends and family and went back to the village the following year to deliver them to the school. Soon after, he quit the corporate world to devote himself full-time to starting Room to Read.

Wood applied his experience as a businessman into his new role as the head of a nonprofit. At the bottom of the Room to Read home page is a line of industry awards and "seals of approval," including a four-star rating from Charity Navigator and a commendation for meeting "Standards for Charity Accountability" from the BBB Wise Giving Alliance (a merger of the National Charities Information Bureau with the Council of Better Business Bureaus). There's also a "bug" for the Social Capitalist award from Fast Company and the Monitor Group, which Room to Read has won four years running in recognition of its innovation and social impact, as well as its business model.

5. Demonstrate your impact.

Endorsements, of course, are not enough. The proof also has to be in the pudding. The marketing message must also match the actual experience of the product or organization.

"Marketing can drive awareness and interest. Marketing can modify behavior and change perceptions. Marketing can build buzz. But that's where the buck stops. What ultimately drives purchase is the sales and customer experience," according to Delia Passi, co-author of *Winning the Toughest Customer: The Essential Guide to Selling to Women*. At the end of the day, your organization has to show results by matching the "marketing promise."

The Room to Read Web site reports on donors' return on investment by quantifying its impact: Since its founding in 2000, the organization has improved the lives of over 1.2 million children worldwide by establishing 3,600 libraries in countries including Sri Lanka and India. Like Save the Children, it accounts for its spending, with slightly more than 90 percent to programs.

Kiva is another nonprofit that does a scrupulous job of enabling donors to follow the money.

Nonprofit Case Study: **Kiva and the Power of Micro-Loans**
Since 2005, Kiva has been an online connector between donors and entrepreneurs in developing countries seeking loans so they can take their small businesses to the next level. When you visit www.kiva.org, you can scroll through a list of profiles to select the business owner you want to support. When we last checked, there was a woman who wanted to expand her business selling rice and Khmer food in front of her house in Phnom Penh; a man in Peru who recently started up his own auto body repair shop; and the mother of five children in rural Pakistan seeking a loan to buy a new cow to grow her thriving milk-selling business.

On the Web site, Kiva keeps a running tab for each loan-seeker of how much has been raised to date, and how much more is needed. Once you make a loan or donation, you'll receive periodic updates from the business you've sponsored. And once the loan is repaid, you can choose to withdraw your funds or loan it out to another entrepreneur. All the business owners are vetted by a network of Kiva's on-the-ground microfinance institutions.

Demonstrating the Impact of Advocacy

Not every nonprofit provides this type of direct service, which can make quantifying results trickier. Those of us who do advocacy work to move policy, for example, know what a long haul it can be, with the pay-off sometimes years away. The trick here is to keep the momentum and the enthusiasm of your supporters alive by demonstrating incremental progress along the way, whether it's getting media exposure for putting the problem on the public's radar; steadily building alliance support among influential stakeholders; or turning people out for public hearings, town halls, or letter-writing campaigns that show decision makers your growing influence. And of course, if and when you've influenced legislation, celebrate big and let the world know what role you played in making it happen.

Nonprofit Case Study: **Innocence Project:**
200 Exonerated and Counting
As we were writing this chapter, a man named Bryon Halsey became the 200th individual to be exonerated of a crime he did not commit, thanks to new DNA evidence. Halsey served 19 years in a New Jersey prison, wrongfully convicted of assaulting and murdering two children before forensic evidence proved without a doubt that another man had committed the crime.

The organization that helped set Halsey free was the Innocence Project, founded by two attorneys, Barry Scheck and Peter Neufeld. Since the duo began studying and litigating on cases involving the use of DNA testing nearly 20 years ago, their groundbreaking work has helped galvanize the debate on the death penalty. With each highly publicized exoneration, public consciousness rises regarding the accuracy and reliability—or lack thereof—of eyewitness identification, false confession, and a host of other factors that routinely contribute to wrongful convictions. As the cases themselves—heartbreaking stories of innocent men who have spent 10, 15, to 20 years behind bars—keep the issue in the headlines and stir public outrage and concern, they also provide the Innocence Project with a high-profile countdown to reform.

The organization's Web site (www.innocenceproject.org) includes a link, "Fix the system," which describes their efforts to reform the criminal justice system and law enforcement procedures. The link provides information on model legislation the group has advanced on everything from compensation statutes for the wrongfully convicted to laws protecting and preserving forensic evidence.

Connecting the Dots between Political Giving and Social Change

When the Women's Campaign Forum Foundation began researching women's political and cause-driven giving habits, they uncovered some fascinating fissures in donor behavior. Women's political giving was generally lower compared to men, but dollar contributions increased for issue-related political action committees (PACs), and even more so for charitable organizations. In other words, when it comes to giving, women are more likely to trust that their dollars are better put to work by supporting issue-based organizations versus political candidates.

What's going on here? For starters, it's worth noting that the Federal Election Commission does not track smaller donations of $200 or lower, which accounts for a large chunk of women's political giving. These female-driven small donations also account for the smash success of EMILY's List, the largest PAC in the nation. Meanwhile, groups like MoveOn.org that raise millions from modest but mass donations of $10 to $50, and political candidates like Senator Barack Obama whose $25 fundraisers helped popularize his support, have cashed in with this savvy "strength in numbers" approach.

Beyond this "power of many" phenomenon, however, there are other forces at work worth analyzing more deeply. As we've shown in earlier chapters, women are not shy about opening up their wallets when it comes to supporting causes and organizations they believe in. Yet for women, there's a disconnect between political candidates and the issues they're passionate about, which translates to a gap between political giving and charitable giving.

The Women's Campaign Forum Foundation's research revealed that many charitable female donors are not aware of how elected officials might advance their causes, by awarding budgetary dollars, passing or blocking legislation, or helping to raise the visibility of their issues. Yet these charitable donors, by virtue of their willingness to give for change, clearly represent a goldmine of potential political giving converts, provided they are cultivated in the right way.

"Our research found that many women don't necessarily connect candidates to advancing the issues that matter most to them—whether it's healthcare, jobs, or education," said Ilana Goldman, president of the Women's Campaign Forum Foundation. "When I talk to women who've never written a check to a candidate, I often put it this way: You could give $50 to your favorite breast cancer organization, or you can give that same amount to elect a candidate who will then advocate for a $50 million appropriation for breast cancer research. In other words, if you already vote and give to causes, political giving is another way you can actively invest in the change you want to see in the world."

What's needed is nothing short of a culture shift in how candidate campaigns and political action groups approach women for their political dollars. This involves changing women's perception about political giving so they see it as a vehicle for making social change, alongside voting and volunteering.

"We must make the case to women that politics matter and who we have in office at every level impacts their lives and the lives of their families," said Andrea Dew Steel, one of the biggest-dollar female Democratic donors in country, and political advisor to the Susie Tompkins Buell Foundation. "If women start giving more money, we will also see more women running for office. Writing a check is often the first step towards full political participation."

Another important finding: women who give to charity also represent the "low hanging fruit" for political fundraisers because they're already putting their money where their issues—and values—are.

A note here on *values*. Many people who respond to public opinion polls will say that they base their vote on the bread-and-butter issues. But we believe the candidate's values are equally important for swaying votes. Values are part of the "vision thing" that brands a candidate, more so, we would argue, than any policy proposal on any particular issue, whether it's healthcare or the environment. Indeed, behind every policy proposal are values, and it's the broad brushstroke of *values* that often moves people to vote for one candidate over the other. By aligning your candidacy closely to the values you believe in, you're helping women (and men) connect the dots between what you stand for and what you'll do on the issues that matter most to them.

For the 2008 election, the Women's Campaign Forum Foundation has taken its own research to heart by organizing a series of regional forums across the country designed to bring more women face-to-face with the candidates. At these forums, women will learn about the issues, and just where the candidates stand on them.

6. Make her feel part of a group effort.

As we've described in previous chapters, when women know that they are acting as part of a community that is contributing to something greater than themselves, women are motivated to give.

The same principle applies to both charitable and political giving. Female political donors who took part in focus groups commissioned by the Women's Campaign Forum Foundation said they were inspired to give by knowing a candidate, knowing people who supported them, and being part of a movement.

While this desire for greater involvement in giving may be an inherent part of female gender culture, it has also come to define a growing trend within philanthropy. According to the *New York Times*, thousands of donors today are "thinking beyond checkbook philanthropy" by rolling up their sleeves and taking a more active approach to understanding how the beneficiaries of their giving operate and determining where specifically they want their money to go.

While average donors can't take fact-finding trips to Africa like Bill and Melinda Gates, they have access to many other avenues. Nonprofits and political campaigns can help by providing more opportunities for donors and would-be donors to immerse themselves more intimately with their work and their candidates.

For political fundraisers, these opportunities can involve creating more forums, such as regional issue summits, for women to meet candidates face-to-face and talk about the policy issues that matter to them most.

Nonprofits can consider holding periodic "open houses," talks, or small briefings for donors to meet staff in a setting that fosters a more intimate back-and-forth exchange. A number of groups that work on international issues will also sponsor special donor delegations to regions abroad where they do program work. If you don't have the resources to send donors on trips, consider bringing the trip back to them in the form of talks that accompany photo exhibits or video. Keeping a blog of your travels can also provide members and supporters with a virtual "real time" front seat to your experiences.

World Vision, for example, hosts a blog (http://wvus.blogspot.com) that features journal entries from its field staff from across the world. When World Vision's U.S. Web editor Larry Short recently took a week-long trip with his daughter to the Democratic Republic of Congo (DRC), his blog gave a vivid account of their experiences. The entries covered everything from the "horns honking, goats bleating, taxi drivers calling out for fares" in the bustling city of Lubumbashi to a visit to a special school for deaf-mute children in the Katanga Province.

According to Short's blog entries, the school was raising money to build on-campus dormitories because many of the students had to walk as many as 20 miles to get to the school, and more than one child walking on country roads had been hit by vehicles they could not hear in the pre-dawn darkness. In his colorful accounts, Short opened a window onto the types of projects World Vision funds so donors could "see" for themselves the enormous need—and considerable impact—their dollars can make in the DRC .

The Rise of Giving Circles

Some women haven't waited for movements to come to them; they've created their own by founding or joining giving circles in their local communities. Giving circles, an exciting and growing trend within philanthropy driven initially by women but expanding more and more to include men, are groups of individuals who pool their money and decide together to which organizations they'll donate their money..

The first giving circles came about in the early 1990s, but most have formed since 2000, according to a recent study by the Forum of Regional Associations of Grantmakers. The Forum has identified more than 400 giving circles in nearly every state in the country, ranging from the small (the five-person One Percent for Moms in Brooklyn) to the large (Washington Women's Foundation in Seattle, which has 400 members and a four-person staff). It's estimated that in the past four years, giving circles have given nearly $100 million to charity, most of it going to non-profit organizations in their backyards and often to smaller grassroots groups with innovative ideas that don't receive support from mainstream philanthropy.

Giving circles have proven especially popular for individuals who have not traditionally been part of, and have been overlooked by, main-stream philanthropy—women, people of color, young people, and generally speaking, individuals who can't afford to write $10,000 checks. As the study observed, "Giving circles are democratic. Anyone can start one. Anyone can join one." Researchers have also proposed that the circles were a natural outgrowth of our increasingly isolated society, offering people an opportunity to engage their broader community and connect with others through learning, giving, and collective decision-making, often in their own living rooms.

So who's joining giving circles? The Forum collected detailed surveys from more than 160 giving circles, and here's what they found out:

- 81 percent of giving circle participants are women; 19 percent are men. Yet participation among men is growing, with co-ed circles representing 47 percent of the total.

- 13 percent of giving circle donors are people of color—African American, Asian American, and Latinos.

- 59 percent of giving circle donors are between the ages of 40 and 65, although 26 percent of the circles are made up entirely or mostly of donors under 40.

The number of giving circles has doubled in just two years (2004 to 2006), spurred by people's enthusiasm for a brand of philanthropy that provides them with opportunities for community-building and social networking. As women come to play a more dominant role in charitable giving, the popularity of giving circles (which meet so many of the criteria that inspire women's participation) will in all likelihood continue to grow and become a permanent arm of community-based philanthropy.

What's more, as giving circles mature, their passion for giving greater amounts of money only grows. The Forum of Regional Grantmakers study found that half had ramped up the amount of money they gave each year and nearly 40 percent had increased the number of grants awarded, which they did by increasing their members, increasing the giving levels for donors and soliciting outside sources of funding from corporations and foundations.

Beyond increased giving, giving circles are also a catalyst for other forms of giving back and civic engagement. Among giving circle participants surveyed by the Forum, 65 percent volunteered in their communities; 43 percent served as members of nonprofit boards of directors;

40 percent offered some level of "in kind support" (resources or services other than money); and 32 percent of survey respondents said they offered technical assistance in the form of pro-bono legal services and financial and marketing advice to the nonprofits they supported.

Giving circles represent an important prospect for political fundraisers. These built-in networks are already keen on educating themselves about social change opportunities. You could plug in by offering to make a presentation, or inviting them to political events. While you may not get financial return immediately, remember that women rely on peers and other social contacts for advice on what—or who—to support with their votes or their dollars. Research has also shown that giving circle members make it a point to broaden their networks to more prospective donors.

> Philanthropic Case Study: **Women Donors Network**
>
> Founded in 1991, the Women Donors Network (WDN) includes more than 150 women philanthropists who each donate $25,000 or more a year to both domestic and international causes. Today, the total of the Network's charitable gifts rivals some of America's largest foundations.
>
> We interviewed Donna Hall, the network's president and CEO, to get the inside scoop:
>
> *Why join a "women" donors' network? What will you get from the network that's different from other philanthropic opportunities?*
> Donna: "Women are attracted to WDN because they seek community with like-minded women who share their values, their vision, their ability to give at a high level. They find a safe space, free from solicitation, where they can get advice and consulting about their charitable work, where they can learn about the issues that are cutting edge, and where they can leverage power and access to have a more significant impact in the world.
>
> "We focus on building this intimate and safe community, on providing education and in building opportunities through joint funding, both within WDN and in partnership with other organizations that will leverage our power and our money."
>
> *Do you believe giving circles like the Women Donors Network inspire people to give, and give more, than if they didn't belong to a philanthropic network?*
> Donna: "Without a doubt, a very high percentage of our members state that their funding increases when they participate in WDN. I can tell you a

story about a woman who recently inherited money, felt overwhelmed and frightened, joined WDN, and within two years was doubling her giving. She was out and about as a more public speaker, and becoming a real activist for the first time in her life."

How would you characterize the Women Donors Network's members?
Donna: "Our members are very unique. Many come from significant inherited wealth, others have earned wealth, and some have married wealth. They range in age from 20-something to 70-something. They are from all over the country, they hold a variety of political views, but they are all united by our relatively tight-knit community where they feel they can discuss anything, explore anything, and ask anything.

"Their combined giving (not just through WDN, but all their giving in aggregate) is well over $100 million a year, not counting their political giving, which is growing exponentially. In the 2004 elections, we estimated that our members made political contributions exceeding $10 million. In other words, they are a force to be reckoned with and their confidence in their power is growing exponentially."

Conclusion

The old ways of doing business when it comes to raising money and building support, particularly among women, may no longer apply, if they ever really did. Innovation is required, and it's being driven by both nonprofits that are in tune with women's 360-degree lens on decision making and individual donors who want to be more involved in how their contributions are spent.

The spontaneous growth of giving circles is a testament to how women have driven a culture of connection. In this new giving culture, people come together in groups to educate themselves and support a cause, which research has shown has the effect of extending and expanding philanthropy among its members. Women aren't interested in solving the world's problems alone. They recognize it will require committed individuals working together, and are eager to pitch in as part of this group effort.

Women are also driving the trend of combining volunteerism with financial contributions, and in the process, creating the type of loyalty to their favorite causes and organizations that most nonprofits dream of cultivating. Simply put, women don't give the same way men do. The sooner we come to see that as an asset rather than a deficit, the better positioned we'll be to take advantage of this new force in philanthropy and political giving.

Now that we've taken a look at how to unlock women's potential as change makers, we'll spend the next chapter exploring how to make these marketing principles work in women's busy, day-to-day lives.

Chapter Take-Aways

- Women are more thorough and exacting than men when it comes to making a decision. This means the more transparent and forthcoming you are with information that addresses their concerns, the more likely you'll win their support.

- Women may take longer to sign on the dotted line, but when they do, their loyalty and commitment is golden.

- Women are twice as likely as men to make referrals. The exponential value of their word-of-mouth potential makes cultivating them worth it.

- Six concrete strategies for cultivating women's support:

  1. Think long-term.

  2. Don't just ask for money.

  3. Show where the money goes.

  4. Leverage third-party validators.

  5. Demonstrate your impact.

  6. Make her feel part of a group effort.

7

Control

Women as Air Traffic Controllers

In the mid-1980s, Janet Jackson came out from under her brother's shadow and shed the doe-eyed waif she played on *Good Times* with her breakthrough anthem *Control*. In her take-no-prisoners shoulder pads, Jackson sang about taking ownership of her life, on her own terms.

Women in America today are in a similar place. As we've described in previous chapters, thanks to major political and economic milestones over the past four decades, more women today are going head-to-head with men on the job. And they're demanding more parity in the home (albeit with mixed results).

While the news media buzz about women struggling to "have it all" by balancing work and family, most women are simply too busy living the reality to have time to spare worrying about how to make it happen. It's a daily feat that women pull off largely by maintaining a strong sense of control. This doesn't mean all women's struggles are equal—the day-to-day concerns of a poor single mom working two jobs can't compare to a stay-at-home mom living in a wealthy gated community. And it doesn't mean women are perfect—the laundry piles up and dinner may be pizza on some nights. But on the whole, when you talk to women, they'll tell you they're holding things down and proud of it.

For nonprofit organizations, this sense of accomplishment and control can be an enormous asset. As we've shown in the previous chapter, just because women are busy doesn't mean there isn't room in their hearts and minds for a cause that really moves them. But as corporate marketing experts will tell you, successful communications means marketing to "all of her lives." This chapter is about how to navigate women's busy realities so you break through—not with a sledge hammer, but with constructive tools that allow them to make time and bandwidth for your issues.

1. Put her in the driver's seat. Women are used to managing their own lives and often the lives of their families, so when it comes to making social change, they naturally look for opportunities to make a difference by taking charge and making a meaningful contribution. They also want assurances that it's possible to move the needle.

2. Parachute into her reality. To stay on top of their busy lives, women have adapted by becoming skilled multi-taskers. Nonprofits seeking to recruit their support can adapt, too, by finding ways to make their lives easier while educating them about the issues.

3. Give her news she can run with. Appeal to a woman's hunger for information and practical approach to getting things by providing her with hands-on information related to your issue that she can translate into her own life to make change.

It's no coincidence that the metaphors we're using in this section reflect bodies in motion. Women are on the go—and if you want to be along for the ride, you have to adapt to the road conditions.

1. Put her in the driver's seat.

Debbie Downer vs. Erin Brokovich

Debbie Downer is a recurring character on *Saturday Night Live* who has a knack of bringing down the mood of everyone around her with her negative observations about the state of the world. Her theme song says it all:

> *You're enjoying your day*
> *Everything's going your way*
> *Then along comes Debbie Downer.*

Let's face it, sometimes the nonprofit sector can be something of a Debbie Downer. We don't do this on purpose. When we tell people that, in the next 20 years, more than two-thirds of the world's population will experience water shortages, we do so out of a sense of urgency. When we say that ocean pollution and over-fishing will lead to the extinction of seafood in less than 50 years, it's because we want people to pay attention before it's too late.

But this "sky is falling" approach can produce unintended and unproductive side-effects. Faced with such dire prognoses of our future on this earth, people start to tune out and numb down, succumbing to a serious case of compassion fatigue. We're already so busy with our personal and professional lives, taking on an "issue"—especially one that doesn't seem winnable—can feel overwhelming.

So who, and what, is the antidote to Debbie Downer?

Try Erin Brokovich.

Brokovich managed to bring Pacific Gas and Electric Company (PG&E) to trial for contaminating groundwater in a small town in California and win a $333 million settlement—the largest settlement in U.S. history ever paid in a direct-action lawsuit. Her story, of course, became part of popular culture thanks to the 2000 movie starring Julia Roberts in the title role.

Erin was an Everywoman heroine: a former beauty queen and single mom of three kids who, at the beginning of the movie, is down to $74 in her bank account. Yet, without any formal legal training, she goes up against the Establishment—not to mention a condescending boss—armed with just her brains, dogged persistence, and chutzpah, and scores one for the people.

Audiences, including women, loved it. Other movies, including *Norma Rae, Thelma and Louise, Silkwood*, and even *Double Jeopardy* with Ashley Judd (a modestly budgeted thriller that stunned Hollywood when it topped the box office for three weeks and grossed over $100 million) have clicked with female audiences, who swiftly translated word of mouth to ticket sales.

The success of these movies reflects the enormous hunger among women for empowered heroines who know how to take charge of tough situations—and kick butt. We cheer them on against the odds. And we rejoice in their victory. Women want to see heroes, and themselves, in the driver's seat. Nonprofits, take note.

Many issue campaigns we encounter actually do have a message of empowerment and hope to share, but this message often gets buried or lost. The trick is finding the right balance. For the most part, political candidate campaigns have learned this lesson already. They know "going positive" on their own platform and vision for the future will often resonate with voters more than going negative on their opponent. Nonprofits can do this, too.

Nonprofit Case Study: **CARE—"I am powerful."**

One organization that takes the empowerment message to heart is the humanitarian organization CARE. The first thing you see when you click on their home page is a portrait of a woman gazing confidently back at you. The headline: "She has the power to change the world. You have the power to help her."

The message underscores CARE's theory of change: the not-so-secret secret to fighting global poverty is to invest in community-based efforts to lift poor women because "equipped with the proper resources, women have the power to help whole families and entire communities escape poverty."

By encouraging people to put power in the hands of women, last year CARE's programs improved the lives of more than 31 million people in Africa, Asia, Latin America, and the Middle East. They improved schools, prevented the spread of HIV, made it easier for people in the developing world to access clean water and sanitation, and helped war-torn and disaster-afflicted communities rebuild economically.

"At CARE, we believe that solidarity amongst women is the answer. If women in wealthy countries like the United States join together with women in the developing world, our world can be changed for the better," said Adam Hicks, Vice President of Marketing and Communication for CARE USA. "We're mobilizing American women to donate, educate, advocate, and volunteer so that their marginalized sisters around the world can realize their innate ability to create different futures for themselves and their children."

Nonprofit Case Study: **Climate Counts**
—"It's 2056. Planet Saved."

From massive floods to drowning polar bears, the drumbeat to Armageddon that is global warming is a test case in doomsday prophesizing.

Climate Counts is an environmental initiative founded by Stonyfield Farms, whose goal is to eradicate global warming. Yet the tone of the campaign is decidedly upbeat and "can do."

Their Web site features a mini-movie that offers a happy ending scenario to the climate crisis titled: "Climate: A Crisis Averted." The video begins with a *Jetsons*-inspired cityscape of the future, where an above-ground tram speeds by, powered by wind generators. A voice-over reports that, between 2006 and 2016, people worldwide took the problem of global warming into their own hands by finding environmentally friendly alternatives to fossil-fuel consumption. Major corporations followed suit: Ford introduces the "H," the first mass-produced hydrogen car. McDonald's gets into the biodiesel business by converting cooking oil to "McFuel." The piece ends on a motivational note, "We dreamed the change. And it happened."

The site also features a "Carbon Calculator" that lets you figure out your own CO_2 footprint based on the vehicle you drive and your home heating and electricity use, and then offers action tips you can take to offset your global warming impacts. To help guide your shopping decisions, you can download from the site a pocket card that scores companies' commitments to reduce global warming pollution.

"The overarching message is that a better future is possible, and we—with women and children leading the charge—can secure it," said Climate Counts' executive director Wood Turner. "But to enlist their support, we knew it was important to avoid terrifying language and imagery and to be very solutions-oriented. Women have demonstrated their desire time and again to share real solutions throughout their networks, and in the early stages of Climate Counts, we have benefited from that same energy and passion.

"In the age of information overload, women are critical to making sense of it all," noted Turner. "We have seen them become societal filters—they help to tune out the noise to determine what's really good and motivational, and they have a deep sense of responsibility for sharing high-quality, largely positive information with their family, friends, and neighbors. At Climate Counts, we revere women as mavens of good."

2. Parachute into her reality.

Here's what we mean by "her reality": During her lunch break, she stops by the department store to pick up a Father's Day gift. Between memos and meetings, she picks up her child from day care. She grades papers on her subway ride home. Spare time means another opportunity to get things done, for herself and for the people in her life. The nonprofit that understands this action-packed reality and finds a way to help it hum even more smoothly will earn a woman's gratitude—and a second look.

"Nonprofit organizations can pry this window open a lot wider by packaging information in a way that taps in women's multi-tasking mind frame," said Holly Minch, vice president at Spitfire Strategies, who echoes Celinda Lake's advice to offer women "two-fors"—a two-for-one package of your "ask" along with something related to your issue that also has a practical or just-for-fun use in women's lives.

Give Her a Two-For

Corporate marketers are geniuses when it comes to the two-for. Think about those "free" goodie bags cosmetic companies give out when you buy a certain amount of their products. Never mind that most of the time you don't end up wearing the lipstick they give you. Everyone could use a free gift once in a while. National Public Radio, for example, has this down cold in their fundraising drives, offering tote bags, magazine subscriptions, and other freebies with your contribution.

Below are two other two-for campaigns we like from the nonprofit sector:

Nonprofit Case Study: **Project Kid Smart**—*Mary Had a Little Amp*
Among the many transformations that come with parenthood is a radical shift in the kind of music you find yourself popping into the CD player in your car. Hip hop and Indie rock get replaced by toddler-friendly sing-a-longs.

Julie Burton, director of Project Kid Smart, had this in mind when she came up with an idea for a two-for to raise awareness and support for voluntary preschool education for all. With consulting partners, she produced a benefit CD, featuring children's songs by Maroon 5, R.E.M., the Dixie Chicks, and Madonna and sold it in record stores across the country and through major internet outlets through a partnership with Sony BMG Music Entertainment. All proceeds went to support Project Kid Smart's advocacy work and public awareness work for state and national legislation like the *Smart from the Start Preschool Education Fund for America* that would designate $5 billion over five years to help states jumpstart the process of providing voluntary preschool for all kids.

Consumers who bought *Mary Had A Little Amp* were driven to the organization's Web site, where Burton greeted them with a personal note that took into account parents' busy lives: "Time is a precious commodity for busy parents. Our site is built around short, concise fact sheets and summaries of important research on preschool education."

She also got the "control" thing down: "We are building a movement for preschool education. We know information is power and we hope to give parents, educators, and advocates the research-based facts and information they need to advance this important campaign."

Nonprofit Case Study: **Ploughshares Fund** — **Rediscover Mother's Day**

The venerable peace group Ploughshares Fund recently sponsored a fund-raising and awareness campaign tied to Mother's Day. Very few know that Mother's Day originated as "Mother's Day for Peace" and was conceived by a suffragist and abolitionist named Mary Ward Howe, whose other claim to fame was writing the words to the *Battle Hymn of the Republic*. She conceived the holiday to spread the message of peace after witnessing firsthand the horrors of the Civil War.

As part of its Rediscover Mother's Day campaign, Ploughshares invited people to put the peace back in Mother's Day by sending e-cards that do the double duty of passing on Howe's vision of peace and connecting with mom on Mother's Day. Ploughshares also set up a partnership with Organic Bouquet to offer a free bouquet of flowers with a contribution of $250 or more to the organization.

The campaign, which included an aggressive online marketing campaign and media outreach, raised a total of $226,080. Online donations, the majority of which were made by first-time donors, accounted for more than $29,000. The campaign also got a huge $100,000 boost from Julia's Circle, a giving circle of 10 mothers from around the country who each pledged $10,000. And a simultaneous online petition campaign on the Care2 Web site in the month leading up to Mother's Day helped generate over 20,000 new signups for Ploughshares Fund's newsletter and fundraising appeals.

It's the Little Things that Count

Most nonprofits don't have access to world-famous recording artists or the resources to release a CD. But don't let that stop you. Little things can count, too. For example, People for the Ethical Treatment of Animals (PETA) gives away vegan and vegetarian recipes on its Web site. The thing to remember is, when you ask for a little, see if there's a way that you can give a little, too, by making a woman's life that much easier and brighter.

3. Give her news she can run with.

Sometimes good information can be as valuable, indeed, *more* valuable, than a goodie bag. Swag has a shelf-life, but knowledge is forever.

As we described earlier in this book, a woman is an indefatigable seeker when it comes to finding advice and practical tips on how to live her life better, or make her life easier. And she's not just looking for herself, but for the others in her life who, whether they know it or not, depend on her for similar information, especially when it comes to health.

Corporations do this kind of stuff all the time. Hamburger Helper offers recipe ideas right on the box. Last year, Timberland Shoes began featuring the social and environmental equivalent of a nutrition label on its shoeboxes by answering the question, "What kind of footprint will you leave?" Each label provides an account of what went into the making of a pair of Timberlands, from how much energy per kilowatt hour per day was used for manufacturing to where the shoes were made and the factory's compliance with labor standards and nondiscriminatory codes of conduct.

These are examples of news you can use—information that may not relate directly to your issue or product, but that helps people translate the essence of your cause to practical purpose in their own lives. This translates to good marketing and often strong word of mouth for your organization.

Another example that we've passed along through word of mouth ourselves is www.askpatty.com because it gives good information and offers a brilliant case study in how to market to women effectively.

Corporate Case Study: **AskPatty.com**

Women buy half of all the new cars and trucks sold in the United States, but that purchasing power hasn't necessarily translated to equal treatment at many car dealerships where women still get the short end of the stick shift.

As an answer to the strain of chauvinism in the automotive world, Jody DeVere founded www.Ask Patty.com, a Web site that bills itself as "safe place" for women to get advice on buying or maintaining their cars. Women can submit questions to "Patty" (staffed by an advisory board of female automotive experts) via email or through the site's interactive blog on everything from how often to replace a timing belt to how to negotiate a lease.

The site is also a database, searchable by zip code and car brand, of "female friendly" certified dealers across the country. Another regular feature

is 20-minute podcast "womanars" on topics like what to look for when purchasing used vehicles, taught by woman experts like Kim Walker, who owns
Peak Automotive, an independent auto shop in Apex, North Carolina. This
real-person connection helps set AskPatty apart from its competitors, according to DeVere. "It is from women by women, but more than that, AskPatty
is heartfelt. It's not just words and information."

Below are examples of how nonprofit organizations have provided "news
you can use" to their campaign and marketing toolbox:

Nonprofit Case Study: **American Lung Association** **—Stick With the Flu Shot**

Each year, hundreds of thousands of emergency-room visits related to flu
and pneumonia can be prevented if people take the preventative measure
of getting inoculations before flu season begins.

The American Lung Association launched a social marketing campaign
aimed at encouraging people—particularly children and older adults—to
do so. The organization released the requisite report connecting the dots
between flu shots and reducing the risk of serious illness. It also promoted
its cadre of medical professionals to take the message to the airwaves and
newspapers.

But it's one thing to tell people to "stick with the flu shot," and another
to give them concrete tools they can use to help make it happen. That's why,
as part of its campaign, the American Lung Association got the word out
about a new feature on their Web site, a "flu shot locator" that lets people
type in their zip code to find out the nearest health clinic, pharmacy, or
other facility nearest to them that is providing inoculations. The online locator proved to be so popular that the site crashed more than once as millions
of people plugged in. It proved to be a highly successful venture in public
education and social marketing.

Nonprofit Case Study: **Environmental Defense** **—Which Fish is Safe?**

Faith Popcorn and Lys Marigold describe how savvy companies anticipate
their customers' needs even before the customers have defined the need for
themselves. "'Anticipating' means understanding your female customer well
enough without having them draw you a diagram," according to Popcorn,
because, "If she has to ask, it's too late."

A great example of this type of marketing comes from the people at

Environmental Defense. They've created an elegant answer to a question that strikes health and eco-conscious people in the supermarket or at a restaurant, "How do I know if this fish is safe?"

The solution is a buying guide for eco-friendly fish that can literally fold up to fit in your pocket or wallet. Their "Pocket Seafood Selector" runs down a list of "best choices" (abalone and tilapia among them) and "worst choices" (culprits include Chilean sea bass and swordfish) based on their mercury and other contaminant levels and whether they are high in healthy omega-3 fatty acids.

You can download the pocket guide for free from their Web site. The user-friendly tool is not only practical, it serves as a great marketing and branding vehicle for Environmental Defense and its good works.

Nonprofit Case Study: **Everything You've Always Wanted to Know About Sex and Drugs But Were Afraid to Ask**

In 1993, health educators at Columbia University in New York started an online "Dear Abby"-type service, offering students information on everything from relationships, sex, and emotional health to alcohol, drugs, and physical fitness.

Overnight, *Go Ask Alice!* went from generating enormous campus buzz to becoming an Internet sensation, drawing widespread media coverage and an audience that extended well beyond Columbia's student body.

The service, which is staffed by a team of health educators and health care providers at Columbia as well as other health professionals, fields questions as wide-ranging as, "What is Chlamydia?" to "Is it possible to die from a marijuana overdose?"

Go Ask Alice! receives nearly 2,000 questions weekly from college and high school students, parents, teachers, professionals, older adults, and others. The Web site also offers a searchable archive of 3,000 previously-posted questions and answers. The site has won praise from health experts and the media alike. As *Details* magazine noted: "No inquiry is too sick, or too stupid. Alice is smart, funny, non-judgmental, and serves it straight."

FAQs R Us

It can be labor intensive to maintain a weekly rotating Q&A service like *Go Ask Alice!* But don't feel like you have to do it all to do it well. Most nonprofits make it a practice to offer a "Frequently Asked Questions" section on their Web site. But you might also consider providing "Fast

Facts"—interesting, or surprising facts about your issue—or a "tip sheet" that can help ordinary Americans support or be mindful of your cause by doing something proactive and practical in their day-to-day lives.

Conclusion

When those of us in the nonprofit sector think about "service," we almost always exclusively think about service to the targeted populations whose lives we are working to improve. But if another goal is to cultivate support among constituents, we should also think about service to this critical audience. When we address people's needs and their desire to do more than write or sign a petition, we open the door to more active participation. We also brand ourselves as useful resources, which can cut both ways when we call on them to return the favor in support of our cause.

In these past chapters, we've given you some core principles that get at *how* to reach women through marketing. The next part of the book is devoted to helping you zero in on *where* to reach them.

Chapter Take-Aways

- Navigate women's busy realities by:

  —putting her in the driver's seat by giving her opportunities to make a difference by making meaningful contributions with an assurance that it's possible to have impact; and

  —parachuting into her reality by finding ways to make her busy life easier while educating her about the issues.

- Many issues campaigns have messages of empowerment and hope but this message often gets buried by "the sky is falling" headlines. The trick is finding the balance between getting people's attention, communicating a sense of urgency, and convincing people that a solution is possible.

Busy women appreciate a "two-for" offer that marries their commitment to do good with useful and practical information, like gift-giving ideas, health advice, or what to put on the table for dinner.

Part III

Where to Hit the She Spot

8

Where to Reach Women

Where to Pick Up Women

In June 2007 *Time Out New York*, the weekly magazine guide to New York City events, devoted a cover story to single women in Manhattan. One subject of the piece, a 44-year-old attorney named Alice, was asked where she went to meet men.

She responded, "That's part of the problem. I like to do a lot of girl things, and girly events are probably the worst place to meet guys. Right now I'm obsessed with Argentine tango. Last Monday I was at Dance Manhattan—all women."

No doubt, there are plenty of places where you'll find both men and women, but as Alice the attorney can attest, there are also certain spots and activities that tend to attract more women than men. The same goes for media destinations, including which online sources women target for information. If you want to meet women where they are, you need to first find out where they go.

The News Media—Do They Still Matter?

As we write this, the news media landscape is undergoing massive transformation. Most media sectors are losing popularity, nowhere more so than the newspaper industry, where declining circulation and advertising sales are resulting in mass lay-offs at dailies across the country. Meanwhile, audiences for evening network news continue to drop about 1 million a year, as it has for the past 25 years.

Why is this so? Part of it has to do with our changing lifestyles (more on this later) and part of it is driven by the proliferation of alternative news sources, including ones that some in the journalism establishment may not consider "legitimate," at least by traditional definitions. An increasing number of Americans now search the Internet for headlines. More and more Americans, especially 20- and 30-somethings, have abandoned so-called "objective" reporting for news with a point of view (i.e., political blogs, and shows like *The Daily Show by Jon Stewart*, and *The O'Reilly Factor*).

According to the Project for Excellence in Journalism, these competing platforms mean that "Journalism is becoming a smaller part of people's information mix. The press is no longer a gatekeeper over what the public knows."

News consumption, like so many other things we do, has become splintered, part of the quickening ebb of our lives, along with coffee and a bagel to go, errands between meetings, shopping online, and take-out for dinner. For women, the consummate multi-taskers, time (and how little there is of it in a 24-hour day) is the defining factor for how they consume media—and how much they take in at any given sitting. Women are more likely than men to scan, rather than consume a newspaper from beginning to end.

In this go-go environment, does making the eleven o'clock news still matter? The answer is a definitive yes. Many nonprofit organizations seek media coverage for multiple reasons, not the least of which is to reach lawmakers and other important influencers for whom the news remains an essential window on the issues and the concerns of constituents.

And while Americans, particularly women, may have less time to absorb the news, the media remain an important source of information. One in four women (25 percent) ages 25 to 54 cite media reports as the most credible source of information, compared to three percent for direct mail and two percent for advertising. Women also give special credence to individuals they perceive as experts (27 percent). Given the "king-maker" effect that the news media can have in choosing experts as commentators on the news of the day, getting your organization's spokespeople quoted and on the air is critical.

What you do with your air time is as important as getting it in the first place. Women report that they have much more on their minds than they did five years ago, and competition for their attention is fierce. This means as communicators, we have to be even more disciplined about maximizing our window of opportunity. From a messaging perspective, it means making an iron-clad connection between our issues and how they affect the people in a woman's life and community—the people for whom she filters information.

It's worth noting that people's attention span for the news expands during election season as they turn to the media for insight into the candidates. Nearly two-thirds of voters in the 2001 election said televised presidential debates were influential in helping them decide who to cast their ballot for—up from 41 percent of those surveyed in the 1996 election. Watching the debates was more influential for women than for men in helping them make up their minds (66 percent vs. 58 percent).

What's more, online news during the elections has gained ground as a go-to source. Twice the number of Americans went online for election news in 2006 than did so in the previous 2002 mid-term elections, part of the general rising trend of news consumption during election season.

And before you write print journalism off, consider this: two-thirds, or 66 percent of people who follow political news closely, prefer newspapers over the next most popular medium, network news, by a full 20 percentage points. This, of course, is important for nonprofits that do advocacy and/or research on legislative issues, given that individuals who follow politics are more likely to be politically engaged and take action on behalf of the causes close to their hearts.

News Consumption: The Gender Split

Television News

Television remains the most popular news source for half of all Americans, and for women in particular. In the morning and daytime hours, you're more likely to find women getting their news from the tube, while more men rely on the radio. At mid-day, nearly half (47 percent) of all women turn on the TV news, compared to 34 percent of men. In the evening, more women than men watch a nightly network newscast on CBS, ABC, or NBC, whereas just a few years ago there was little to no gender gap in network news viewership.

The Pew Research Center for People and the Press:
The News Gender Gap

Regularly read, watch, listen to	Men %	Women %	Difference
Newspaper	47	37	−10
Radio News	45	36	−9
News Online	33	25	−8
Cable News	41	35	−6
Local TV News	56	61	+5
Nightly Network News	30	37	+7
Network News Magazines	17	26	+9
Network Morning Shows	16	28	+12

Radio News

As the table above illustrates, radio is where you'll lose women, and the split becomes even more pronounced in the arena of commercial news/ talk radio, where male listenership has an even greater edge. The exception is public radio, where the genders tend to balance out more, with a listenership that is 52.5 percent male and 47.5 percent female.

Men are also more likely to consume the new digital audio options, making up 58% of the population who listen to radio online. Other new audio formats are more balanced between the sexes, though still tilt toward men: satellite radio attracts an audience that is 53% male and 47% female, and podcasting splits 52% male and 48% female.

Online News

Over the past few years, online news consumption has grown steadily across every major demographic group, although this growth leveled off in 2006, according to the latest research by the Pew Research Center for People and the Press.

The growth has been particularly pronounced among men, with fully 20 percent of American men naming the Internet as their most important news source, although women's reliance on online news has also climbed steadily. The dominant sites for online news seekers are Yahoo News, followed by MSNBC, CNN, and AOL News, although television-news Web sites are gaining ground. News executives are paying attention to consumer trends by beefing up their online news staff.

Connecting With Women in Cyberspace

As we described earlier, people today are getting information from many more sources than traditional news outlets. Primary among them is the Internet. In many ways, the Internet was made for women. As a convenient 24/7 treasure trove of information, the Worldwide Web has become an essential tool in many women's on-the-go lives. Little wonder then that in the U.S., women outnumber men online by a significant margin (97 million women compared to 90 million men), even though, as noted earlier, men outnumber women when it comes to seeking *news* online.

This trend is only expected to continue. According to market research firm eMarketer, by 2011, 109.7 million U.S. females are expected to go online, about 51.9% of the total online population. Currently, young women are more likely to be online than young men, and black women in particular are going online in greater numbers.

But for women, the Internet is more than an in-and-out means to an end. Beyond email, they also use it as a platform to communicate with others, whether it's with other users online or with the host organization. This desire and willingness to engage socially has important ramifications for the design and offerings you build into your Web site so that you first attract women, and then keep them there longer.

Marketing expert Allison H. Fine credits the rise of the Internet as a major force of today's "Connected Age" to women, who are driving this sea change with their innate ability to share information and collaborate. According to Fine, "Social media also fits into the lives of working women much better than traditional communications tools. You can work the night shift and respond to email in the morning. You can have four kids and read a blog during naptime."

Marketing to Women Online

A recent British study of Web users found that men tended to favor pages designed by men, and women found sites made by women more appealing. Women, for example, preferred pages with more color in the background and candid, informal photographs rather than staged ones. Men were more disposed to favor dark colors and straight, horizontal lines across the page and a three-dimensional look.

The take-away? Not all Web sites are born equal, as in equally appealing to men and women. For most nonprofits, this means striking a balance to make sure that you're not isolating one gender by unintentionally speaking exclusively to another. But there's no need to over-think it: you won't need one Web site for men and another for women and you don't need to be a female Web designer to create one that appeals to women.

Think of the home page of your Web site as your 24/7 store-front. Marketing experts will tell you that you have less than eight seconds to engage visitors and get them clicking. If she doesn't "get" who you are and what you do in those first few critical moments, she'll be on to her next search.

Below are 11 general but important online marketing tips to keep in mind if you want to appeal to female audiences. Many of them appeal to men, too.

1. Make it matter.

"It" in this case is your mission and your issue or issues. If you want a woman to contribute her time and money to your cause, you have to first convince her that your cause is important in her life and connected to her values and concerns. On the first page of your Web site answer the question, "Why should she care?" Tell her who or what is at stake, why the situation is urgent and what she can do about it.

Tips for Politicians: While it's true that women want to know about you, they're equally (if not more) interested in what you'll do for them and their communities on the issues they care about most. A Web site that's all about the politician, with no images or stories about connecting or interacting with real people, is a turn-off.

2. Keep your navigation simple.

As you're designing or redesigning your Web site, put yourself in the shoes of a woman who may be checking your site during a 15-minute break at work, while her child is sleeping, or while something's cooking on the stove. Searching for information should feel intuitive, including the links to major buckets on your homepage. Also, make it easy for her to navigate back to your home page or her last search. If you can, have friends or family—not just the technology people—test drive the site before it goes public so you can get real-world feedback on how well it works.

3. Make sure someone's home.

Not literally, of course. But we do recommend that you make sure that visitors can easily find the organization's contact email, phone number, and address on your home page. Not every organization may want to take the extra step of making individual emails public for staff members, but where possible, we think this is an open and friendly touch.

4. Get personal.

Women are more likely than men to click on a site's "About Us" page. This is one of many opportunities your site has to make a human connection, either by telling the story of how your organization began, or by telling the stories of the people whose lives you're working to improve. You can do this through straight content or through audiovisual clips. Don't be a faceless organization; be sure to include photographs and background information about your staff so visitors can learn about the dedicated individuals who make your work possible.

5. Feature people.

When Fenton recently advised on a redesign of a Web site for a regional open space district, one of our recommendations was to diversify their images of pristine woodlands and streambeds with pictures of people fishing and enjoying the nature trails. The goal was to provide a graphic reminder of how much people have to gain by having the great outdoors in their backyard. When marketing your Web site to women, pay close attention to the emotions on the faces of the people you feature as images, because women will. Include more than one person so she will be intrigued by the story behind the relationship.

6. Invite her input and help her connect.

Remember that women seek opportunities to share their opinion and connect to others—that's how they demonstrate their investment in the things they care about. Web 2.0 technology, from blogs and message boards to live online interview chats and social networking sites, lend themselves easily to this form of participation. It can also be as easy as writing "We want to hear from you" on your Web site and then providing an email address for immediate feedback. The point is this: make communication a two-way street by listening to what a woman has to say and then connecting her to others.

7. Make joining and actions easy.

If she's interested in what you do, chances are she'd like to stay in touch. But she's also protective of her privacy and wary of being bombarded with information. So when you ask her to sign up, keep the process simple:

- ask for the essential information you need up front (remember, once you've formed a closer relationship you can ask for more specifics);

- assure her that you'll keep her information confidential;

- give her control and choice by offering a check-list of things she can sign up for (newsletters, action alerts, etc.); and

- let her know how often she can expect to hear from you.

Be sure to give her at least one easy thing to do (send a free e-card to a friend, take a poll, rate an idea, etc.) right away, besides giving money. Remember you're collecting information and beginning a relationship for further cultivation.

8. Let others do the talking.

Remember how we described how important third-party validators are to the credibility of organizations? The same is true on your Web site. Women are more comfortable joining a group, writing a check, taking an action if they can see that other people—just like them (think Amazon. com book reviews)—have done the same thing. Make sure to provide third-party testimonials on your Web site. The Global Fund for Women does an excellent job of letting their donors do the talking about why they give on its Web site. They include personal, heart-felt written letters and photos, including profiles of mother and daughter donors.

9. Details matter.

Women are tough customers. They want to know that the organization they intend to support is well managed and efficient. And women who have already supported the organization want to know that, too. On the home page, have a link to a page that transparently outlines the organization's budget. It can be as simple as a pie chart copied from your annual report. You'll score even more points with women if you have Charity Navigators Four Star Rating or the Better Business Bureau Accredited Charity seal, which acts as a seal of approval.

10. Offer the gift of giving.

Women love giving gifts, which represents a huge opportunity for your donation page. Give visitors the option of making a straight contribution, but also of making a donation in someone else's name, with a card to let that special someone know that a good deed has been done on his or her behalf. This is also a great fundraising strategy to tie to holidays. Last Mother's Day, for example, in response to an appeal by the New York Asian Women's Shelter, Lisa C. sent a check in her mother's name and her mom got a thank-you card in the mail.

> Nonprofit Case Study: **Heifer International**
> **—Making Online Giving Easy and Fun**
> Heifer International is one of the best examples of an organization that gives women the "two-for" by allowing them to do good by giving the gift of a water buffalo, a flock of chicks, or a trio of rabbits that will contribute to the livelihood of a family half-way around the world. On its Web site, the group features a gift registry section for those who want to receive "the gift that keeps on giving" and a gift catalog filled with photos of the animals and the people who need them. The site also makes it easy for gift givers to customize and print out a card to send either electronically or by "snail mail" to the recipient.

11. Don't think pink.

A woman's *B.S.* meter is pretty highly tuned. American Airlines recently learned this the hard way when it launched a lavender-colored Web site marketed specifically to female travelers with travel tips that more than a few women found patronizing: "Always bring a little black dress to wear with these heels," was one such nugget of advice from the "Tips From Our Road Warriors" section of the site. In other words, talk to women—don't talk down to them.

> **Playing Games**
> Mobile handheld devices are shaping up to be the next frontier for e-communications, a trend that is already being driven by Generation Y. A surprising factoid: more women play online mobile games like Scrabble and Tetris than men. Women wireless subscribers account for 65 percent of mobile game revenue. As the public sector continues to seek ways to engage members and constituents where they are (particularly young people and young women), mobile gaming that doubles as a public education or social marketing tool may be one direction to go.

The *Bloghersphere*

Among the important trends to emerge from the 2004 elections was the rising legitimacy of political bloggers who received, for the first time, press passes to cover the conventions. According to the latest survey by the Pew Internet & American Life Project, more Americans are reading blogs than ever before: in 2006, 57 million, or 39 percent of online users read blogs, compared to 27 percent the year before. Women are responsible for creating the majority of blogs on the Internet, and they're more likely than men to continue blogging once they've begun. But when it comes to political blogs, men dominate.

In 2007, *Boston Globe* columnist Ellen Goodman did some research into the top 90 political blogs. She found that 42 percent were edited and written by men only, while seven percent were by women only. Women bloggers were out there, Goodman observed, blogging on everything from motherhood to women's issues, but for Goodman, "This is not just about counting, not just about diversity-by-the-numbers. It's about the political dialogue—who gets heard and who sets the agenda."

Various theories have been posited about why this is so. Political blogs are by nature controversial and often adversarial. Women, who are generally more interested in community-building and problem solving than confrontation and competition—the "horse race" aspect of election politics—may simply be turned off. As Goodman noted in her column, the political blogosphere, like other blogging communities, is a tight-knit community, and male bloggers are more likely to link to other male bloggers. That said, the *bloghersphere* remains a relatively young medium, and the window is wide open for women political bloggers to play a more active and influential role.

"Political campaigns are obsessed with influencing a small group of political bloggers, who are mostly men, and mostly concerned with the horse race," said Morra Aarons-Mele, the political director for BlogHer, an online community for women who blog. "Campaigns are missing a big opportunity: there are thousands of women bloggers—with millions of readers—who care about the election and the big issues, and write about them often." These people are your audience; they are the majority of American voters!

Do You YouTube? Women's Online Video Use

There may be more women than men online overall, but when it comes to watching videos online, there are more men than women, according to a recent marketing survey. The reason for this disparity is attributed to the reason women go online in the first place—to do research and get things done. Men, on the other hand, are more likely to surf for entertainment, which explains why they're more likely to visit video sites like YouTube.

Yet male and female online viewing habits are likely to balance out in the near future. According to market analyst Debra Aho Williamson, young women in their teens and 20s do watch online videos in higher numbers than older women. This trend is expected to contribute to a near 20 percent boost in female viewers overall by 2011, putting them at near par with male viewers in the near future.

Social Networking Media: A Woman's Best Friend

Social networking Web sites, or so-called Web 2.0 technology, were made for women, given the incredible opportunities they represent for connecting and creating and maintaining community. Companies like MySpace and Facebook that offer interactive hubs for members to post personal profiles, blogs, photos, music, and video, and opportunities to network with friends and family, have attracted millions of online visitors from across the world.

Facebook, for example, is now the third most popular site after Google and Yahoo, and it attracts more female than male users—56 percent of female students polled use Facebook, compared to 49 percent of male students—according to a recent study.

Social networking sites are widely understood to attract young people, offering an opportunity to reach more than three million college students in any given month in a targeted way that few media outlets are able to match. That said, it's worth noting that older generations are catching on: according to current traffic trends, more than half of MySpace visitors are now 35 or older.

All of which is to say, online social networking is most certainly here to stay, and many businesses have already moved into the women's market by offering female-friendly social media tools. They include BlogHer, an aggregate blog index of nearly 10,000 blogs authored by women, and

TeamSugar, a network for women by women to share content, opinions, stories, and news. There are also a handful of sites aimed specifically at moms, including MotherProof, launched by www.cars.com, that encourage mothers and others to post their reviews of cars online.

Conclusion

If there's one thing to take away from all this research, it's that the era of one trusted source to which America turns for its news and information is dead. The sheer proliferation of choices, coupled with the changing ways we now consume news—often on the go and between activities—means nonprofit organizations and political campaigns will have to be more creative and strategic about connecting with their target groups, including women. Women have distinct habits and preferences that determine which information sources they turn to and which ones they trust. The more you familiarize yourself with their consumer habits, the more successful you'll be at reaching them. This is what strategic marketing is all about.

In Chapter 9 we'll apply a micro-lens to the female population and examine the differences between a few key segments—the ones that are particularly important for the public and political sectors to reach.

Chapter Take-Aways

- When it comes to news consumption, TV is the go-to source for women, who watch more day-time, mid-day, and evening news than men.

- More women are online and blogging than men, although men currently dominate the political blogosphere.

- Online social networking sites were practically made for women, who value community building and staying in touch.

- If you want your Web site to appeal to women, make sure it's easy to navigate and features images and stories of people, including the "face" of your organization. These things encourage women to "plug in" by participating in your online activities, including making donations.

9

Segmenting the Women's Market

Women, One Segment at a Time

Throughout this book, we've generalized about how and why "women believe this" or "women do that." We've used these broad brushstrokes simply to highlight gender differences—differences between men and women's thinking and doing. In this chapter, however, we put away generalizations to bring forward some of the finer details and differences among women themselves.

Women self-identify along many lines, not just their gender. Racial and ethnic differences, age differences, level of education, children or no children, religious affiliation, marital status, and differences in sexual orientation all contribute to creating sub-groups under the broader category of "women." For the purposes of this chapter, we've chosen to focus on the groups that are most likely to be important "gets" for the majority of nonprofit organizations and political campaigns. Specifically, we look at married and single women, mothers, boomer generation women, and women of color. We recognize that this excludes certain segments, including women of other generations and lesbian, bisexual, and transgender people. Each of these groups is deserving of its own market research and we encourage our readers to explore the studies and books that have been written for and about these other segments, just as we plan to continue our own education.

The Rise of Micro-Targeting

In recent years there has been rising interest in the field of market research known as micro-targeting. Micro-targeting has long been used in the business world as a way to predict consumer behavior by drilling down into personal information and behaviors (your marital status, whether you live in a house or an apartment, how many children you have). Micro-targeting entered into the political mainstream in 2004 when it was widely touted as a winning political strategy for President George W. Bush.

In the battleground state of Ohio, for example, data-mining of African American voters found that they wanted to hear candidates explain their positions on education and health care. The Bush campaign messaged accordingly in its direct mail and phone outreach, a departure from its dominant platform of staying the course in Iraq. The targeted strike helped Bush win 16 percent of the African American vote, up seven percentage points from four years earlier, which contributed to his winning the entire state by a two percent margin.

According to Bush strategist Matthew Dowd, this type of political profiling "gave us a way of finding people we couldn't find before. We could get at Bush voters in Democratic precincts, swing precincts and other places we'd never been able to look before."

Most nonprofits don't have the millions needed to bankroll a micro-targeting campaign, but they can still create a marketing, fundraising, or voter mobilization effort that takes into account the central principle behind micro-targeting: the more you know about your target audience, the better you'll be at marketing your cause to them.

Life Transitions as Opportunities

In 1976, the journalist Gail Sheehy created a cultural sensation with the publication of her best-selling book, *Passages*. Until then, child development experts had long defined transitions among youth, from the "Terrible Twos" to the turbulent period of adolescence, but Sheehy's book helped popularize the idea that adulthood was comprised of a series of life stages as well, with each stage representing its own pitfalls and opportunities for growth.

Among the major life-changing stages in adulthood, particularly for women, are:

- College

- Marriage

- Motherhood

- Retirement

- "Sandwich generation" responsibilities: caring for children and parents

- Empty nesting

The private sector has capitalized on these life transitions to sell everything from life insurance and hardwood floors to time-shares and camcorders. Corporate marketing pros understand that, while quality service and products are always appreciated, they can become even more magnified during a life transition where everything is new and unfamiliar. Make a connection with women at one of those pivotal junctures and you'll have won a loyal customer for life.

Nonprofits can also benefit from these transition moments when people's eyes and minds are open to new ideas and options. AARP, of course, is famous for sending out membership cards to people once they hit fifty. Both the right and left offer fellowships and leadership development programs to college students and recent college graduates with the goal of recruiting and training the next generation of thought leaders.

Below we dive into the traits of five important demographic groups and offer recommendations for how to market to them effectively. We owe a special thanks to marketing experts Lisa Johnson and Andrea Learned for their insights on generational marketing. The groups are:

1. Singles vs. Marrieds

2. Mothers

3. Boomer Generation Women

4. Women of Color

1. Singles vs. Marrieds

The Wedding Band Factor—The Marriage Gap

While much has been made about the political influence and voting habits of parents, from soccer moms to NASCAR dads, a voter's marital status is actually the biggest factor in predicting voter preference. And this year, it's single women who are poised to usher in an era of political change.

In fact, the wedding band factor *transcends* other demographic factors, including generational differences and differences in education levels, according to researchers at the polling firm Greenberg Quinlan Rosner. In other words, a 20-something single woman with a bachelor's degree is more likely to vote in sync with a 60-year-old high school-educated widow than with a college-educated *married* woman also in her 20s.

Generally speaking, married women tend to vote conservative, while unmarried women lean progressive. Part of this split is attributed to pure economics. As we touched on in an earlier chapter, single women tend to be less financially secure as a group (twice as many of them have annual household incomes below $30,000 compared to their married counterparts), which makes them more concerned about social issues like healthcare and protecting safety-net programs. In the 2004 presidential race, President Bush beat John Kerry by 15 percentage points among married people. Among single people, Bush lost by 18 percentage points, according to an exit poll by national news media organizations.

The marriage gap isn't a new phenomenon. But in the past few decades, it has steadily increased, from 17 percentage points in the 1984 presidential election to a 32-point gap in the 2006 election. This and other research that have pointed to unmarried women's demand for change suggests that unmarried women may provide the wind Democrats need for 2008 in the same way that white evangelicals helped George Bush win in 2004—provided Democrats and progressives do a good job of reaching and connecting with them.

Reaching Single Women

If there's one single take-away to be had about reaching single women, it's simply this: Just do it.

As the Greenberg study showed, given the voting patterns and political attitudes of single women, they are the number one "get" for progressive candidates (and an important audience for progressive causes as well). Yet even though unmarried women represent the largest progressive voting bloc in the country, the fact remains that married women as a whole have traditionally cast more ballots: 71 percent compared to

59 percent in the 2004 election. We believe a significant reason for the disparity lies in the fact that political campaigns and candidates have historically neglected single women as a constituent and thus have failed to speak specifically and meaningfully to their concerns. If they were to do so, and do so effectively, it's likely more single women would show up on election day.

Below are five marketing tips for connecting with single women:

- **Speak to their desire for change.**

Remember that unmarried women, more than any other demographic voting bloc, are the ones who say they are hungry for change, big time. According to survey research, 78 percent say the country is on the wrong track. The political campaign and nonprofit that convinces them that they can help achieve the large-scale change that single women want to see in the world will be well-positioned to secure their support.

- **Acknowledge strength and independence.**

Single women are making their own decisions and making it on their own. If you reflect your understanding of the pride they take in their self-reliance and ability to take care of business, you will can help them bridge these emotions to helping others in need.

- **Address financial security concerns.**

Whether she's a single mom or an older woman approaching retirement age, a single woman worries about her financial future, more so than a married woman. Financial security isn't her only issue, of course, but it's an important one. Allay this fear and she'll listen.

- **Evoke opportunity.**

Along similar lines, single women know what it's like to be completely self-reliant and responsible for themselves (and in some cases, their kids). They know how tough it can be, which means they also understand the value of opportunity as an essential ingredient in getting ahead, no matter what your circumstances.

- **Don't fall into the *Sex and the City* trap.**

This highly influential HBO series about "sex and the single girl" has contributed to an unfortunate blanket effect on public perception of who single women are. Keep in mind that widows, working-class single moms, and divorced women are all part of the mix and most of them don't have a Manolo Blahnik obsession.

2. Mothers

Mom Power—Hitting the Mother Lode

Becoming a mother is an enormous life transition, and one that a majority of women will experience. At last count, there are 80.5 million moms in America. A full 81 percent of women between the ages of 40 and 44 in America right now have children. Moms represent the most powerful consumer in the U.S. today, responsible for $1.6 trillion in household spending. They can make or break a product—just as they can make or break an election.

As any parent, expectant parent, or baby shower guest knows first-hand, there is a vast consumer industry surrounding mother and child, from Baby Bjorns and breast pumps to "onesies" and diaper cans. But along with the flood of practical purchases that must be made, many moms also experience a flood of new or intensified emotions related to their new care-giving status.

Lisa W. considered herself an environmentalist before she became pregnant with her son Bruno. But during her pregnancy, she found herself increasingly preoccupied with global warming and the scientific claim that we have a 10-year window to take action before the world starts feeling serious fall-out from heat-trapping carbons. She fretted about the world that Bruno would inherit. These concerns, among others, convinced her to use Seventh Generation recycled diapers and Born-Free bottles made from bisphenol A-free plastic. She also found herself unable to read emotionally wrenching books like Joan Didion's *The Year of Magical Thinking*. When she received an email from the mothers' advocacy group, MomsRising.org, about paid family leave law in New York City, she took action on the spot.

The Modern Mothers' Movement

Lisa W. isn't the only mom getting her activist blood up.

A Google search using the keywords, "Mothers for" will pull up hundreds of organizations, everything from "Mothers for Clean Air" and "Mothers for Peace" to "Mothers for Police Accountability." Moms are in nurturing mode, which means they care about health, safety, the environment, and nothing less than the future of the planet.

In their research on the relationship between parenting and political attitudes and voting behaviors, political scientists Laurel Elder and Steven Greene found that moms are more likely to be actively involved in local school politics and other community issues concerning children. They also found in their 32-year analysis that mothers are significantly more liberal than women without children, especially on social welfare issues and the role of government in creating jobs (interestingly, fathers lean considerably more conservative, especially on social values issues, compared to childless men).

In 2007 the *New York Times* published a story about the recent proliferation of mom-based organizing groups including MomsRising.org and Mothers & More. The article acknowledged that many of the issues that concern modern moms are the same that concerned their mothers 50 years ago, except that they have been repackaged as family and work issues rather than "women's issues." But regardless of the packaging, the bottom line is women struggle with the same problems:

"Raised to believe that girls could accomplish anything, these women have reached parenthood, only to find they faced many of the same pay, equity and work-family balance issues that were being fought over decades before. From that awakening, they say, has come the inkling of a new movement."

MomsRising.org, co-founded by two mothers, Kristin Rowe-Finkbeiner and Joan Blades (who also co-founded MoveOn.org), is among a new breed of advocacy groups driven by moms who are focused on affecting policy reforms that will help parents achieve a life-work balance. The group is 100,000 members strong and growing.

"Many of us thought women were getting closer to equal pay for equal work and are shocked to learn there is profound bias in hiring and wages for mothers," said Blades. "Since 82 percent of women become mothers, all of a sudden it is easy to understand why there are so many women and children in poverty, and so few women in leadership.

"Then we look at the reasons why and realize that, as a society, we have the least support for families of the top 20 industrialized nations in the world. Our members are ready to do what it takes to both create cultural change at work and remind our leaders that we need policies that truly support families."

Reaching Mothers

Below are five pointers for marketing effectively to mothers:

- **Value relationships, because she does.**

  Mothers are in bonding mode, not only with their children but with the people closest to them. Moms want their children's lives to be rich with caring, loving people. For many, becoming a parent also triggers an interest in becoming a more active part of a larger community.

  Nonprofits can market effectively to moms (and dads) by tapping into this mind-set. This means tying your issue to the benefits of family, spending time together, and protecting the future for the next generation. On a graphic level, it means featuring photographs or images of families, whether your issue is protecting open space or protecting Social Security benefits. People are at the center of every issue, and the emotional glue that holds people together is relationships.

- **Save her time.**

  We've covered this ground in an earlier chapter as it applies to all women, but it's especially true for mothers. Lisa W.'s friend, Lauren, a young mother of two children, is a huge fan of home-delivery services like FreshDirect and Max Delivery. "When you have kids you have so many more little things to do," said Lauren, who observed that, as a mother, if you don't find shortcuts, "you'll be spending your entire weekend running around getting things done and not spending time with your child."

  As marketing experts Lisa Johnson and Andrea Learned note in their book *Don't Think Pink*, "Customers think in terms of related activities, while companies tend to think in terms of products." Nonprofits can fall into a similar type of tunnel vision when making the "ask" of their constituents or supporters without first considering what they might have to give in return. One very basic thing that nonprofits can give to mothers is *time* by making it fast and easy for them to take action and donate. You can also help them multitask by offering gifts idea-donation combos or activities for their kids (more on this below).

- **Motivate her by invoking her power, not her guilt.**

  Moms are under enough pressure today to raise their kids properly, without having another voice egging them on about how they may not be doing enough. If you want to move her to action, inspire her by putting the power in her hands. MomsRising.org's "The Power of ONEsie" Campaign, for example, has creatively leveraged action at the grassroots by asking moms around the country to decorate baby "onesies" with messages aimed at policymakers ("Paid Family Leave or Bust"). The clothes are then displayed en masse at hot spots around the country to draw media attention and stimulate debate.

- **Don't overdo the "mom thing."**

Research shows that moms are 80 percent more likely to buy a product from a company that recognizes the multiple roles she plays in her life. In other words, moms don't essentialize themselves as mothers. They're also wives, professionals, daughters, and more. Advertising campaigns that acknowledge these dimensions are more likely to succeed; the same goes for nonprofit and political campaigns. The exception to this rule, of course, is if your organization or campaign is exclusively for or about mothers.

Nonprofit Case Study: **NRDC Says:**
"Protect Yourself and Your Family"

An organization that does this skillfully is the environmental group Natural Resources Defense Council (NRDC). Click on their Web site for information on mercury contamination in fish and you'll find tips under the banner, "Protect Yourself and Your Family." Whether the issue is ocean pollution or toxic chemicals, NRDC connects the dots between environmental protection and the well-being and safety of future generations by featuring photographs of children playing on the beach or in a field (which is a lot more inspiring than looking at a toxic waste dump).

- **Connect with her through her kids.**

Moms are often on the look-out for two types of opportunities for their children: vehicles that will help instill values that will last them a lifetime and fun, kid-friendly alternatives to watching TV (bonus points if they learn something). Many nonprofits are in prime position to offer both. By creating programs aimed at children, you get a two-for: a platform for reaching moms through their kids (not to mention their gratitude) and a way of cultivating supporters at an extremely young age, which is pure gold for building brand loyalty.

Nonprofit Case Study: **Trick-or-Treat Campaign**

UNICEF's long-running Trick-or-Treat campaign is a textbook example of this strategy in action. The annual fundraising effort gets children to help children in other parts of the world by raising money door-to-door during Halloween. The campaign Web site includes easy-to-follow steps for getting involved, other fundraising ideas from kids around the country, and special sections for parents and teachers. UNICEF also breaks out the value of each monetary donation (one dollar can immunize a child against measles for life and $12 can buy 20 packets of high-protein biscuits to feed children suffering from malnutrition).

Nonprofit Case Study: **ASPCA's Animaland**

The American Society for the Prevention of Cruelty to Animals has a separate Web site just for kids with cartoon tips on pet care for everything from hamsters to rabbits, and a feature called, "Ask Azuma" that answers kids' animal-related questions such as, "Do tigers have stripes under their fur?" On its home page there are rotating topical features related to big stories in the news (dog fighting, contaminated pet food problems) that capture audience attention. (By the way, the answer is: Yes, tigers have stripes under their fur.)

3. Boomer Generation Women

When we ask our nonprofit clients to describe their core individual donor base, many of them say it's women in their 40s, 50s, and 60s who are cutting them regular checks. This is true whether the organization is dedicated to improving education or saving the rainforest.

Boomer women are also the most likely demographic to respond to direct mail appeals, according to Mal Warwick, chairman of Mal Warwick Associates, one of the nation's leading fundraising professionals. "In direct mail, the donor base is women. For a large majority of nonprofit organizations, the typical direct mail donor is a 60-65 year old woman of relatively modest means with an above-average education."

In many ways, it's not surprising that the 80 million boomer women born between 1945 and 1964 are the financial backbone of today's social change organizations. After all, this is the generation that ushered in the feminist movement and came of age during the Vietnam War, the Watergate scandal, the civil rights movement and many other familiar political touchstones that have come to define the "left" in many people's minds today.

Debunking the Myth of the (Conservative) "Security Mom"

In February 2003, *Time* magazine's political columnist Joe Klein declared that "soccer moms are now Security Moms," and that, to win their vote (and the election), presidential candidates would have to prove they were tough on terrorism. Many of the national media reiterated this argument; both the Bush and Kerry camps messaged and campaigned furiously on the security platform (Dick Cheney's daughter Elizabeth went so far as to refer repeatedly to herself as a "Security Mom" on the campaign trail).

As it turns out, the so-called Security Mom was as elusive as Big Foot—and about as real.

In the March 2007 issue of *Social Science Quarterly*, political scientists Laurel Elder and Steven Greene reported their findings on one of the first comprehensive analyses of the relationship between parenthood and political outlook. Among the questions they sought to answer was, "Do mothers have distinctly different attitudes regarding security issues, and do they vote significantly differently than women without children?"

What Elder and Greene found did not jibe with conventional wisdom. It was assumed that after 9/11, Security Moms, who had historically supported Democratic candidates because of their stance on social issues like education and healthcare, would vote Republican because of the party's traditional hard-line on security. In fact, more mothers voted for the Gore/Kerry ticket than for Bush in 2004 (54.5 percent compared to 45.5 percent). Even more eye-opening, more *non*-mothers voted for Bush than for Kerry (51.6 percent compared to 48.4 percent).

The study found absolutely no "mother gap" on issues concerning defense and security. What they did find was a *gender gap*, with men significantly more likely than women to support increases in spending on defense and the "war on terror."

Yet, according to the researchers, "the frequent use of 'Security Mom' frames in election stories only reinforced the importance of nation security in the campaign. Meanwhile, social welfare issues, the issues for which mothers truly had distinctive political preferences—and for which the public perceives the Democratic party to be stronger—received less attention."

Baby boomers, of course, aren't the only generation on the block, and not the only one that makes a difference when it comes to making social and political change. That said, for the scope of this book, we've chosen to focus on baby boomer women rather than try to address all the different generations (Gen X, Gen Y, and women in their 70s and older) in order to zero in on the core demographic that we believe is the "must get" for nonprofits and political campaigns. This calculation is based on baby boomers' considerable contributions and capacity for current and future giving and volunteer service, as well as their turn-out on election day.

Many corporate marketing campaigns have chosen to target boomer women, too, but primarily for the power of their purse. This wasn't always the case. It wasn't too long ago that women in mid-life were typecast as homemakers or rendered invisible. Today's boomer women are at the peak of their earning potential which makes them prime consumers as well as prime donors. Most are in the workforce and say they intend to stay that way in some capacity past retirement age. What's more, they will most likely end up inheriting and managing the financial assets from their husbands and parents.

Corporate marketing pros are quick to point out that, because the "boom" represents a relatively long spectrum of 18 years (compared to 11 years for Generation X), you will find a broad diversity of life stages and experiences within this age group. Below are a few things to keep in mind about boomer women audiences:

50 is the New 30

Most boomer women are active, healthy, and young at heart; they don't want to be defined by age alone. The empty-nest syndrome that many of them experience when their children leave home for college and work is a transition moment when many women feel simultaneously alone yet rejuvenated with the realization that the many years ahead of them can now be filled with exploration and adventures of their own choosing. For nonprofits, this life stage represents opportunities to inspire their interest in the arts and culture, in outdoor activities and travel.

For many women, this period of their lives is when they get to finally focus on themselves, which is why "personal growth" is such a huge cottage industry for this demographic and why *Oprah*, with its consultant gurus and promise of self-fulfillment and transformation, is so compelling.

Getting Together

According to Carol Osborn of Imago Creative, a marketing agency that specializes in targeting boomer women, empty nesting also triggers the desire for "communal experience" with girlfriends or other social groups. This goes right back to the "Connecting" principle, whereby you build support for your cause or organization by bringing like-minded people together for fundraising, actions, contests, or just plain celebrating. This dovetails naturally with the ethos of connectedness that we described in Chapter 5.

Taking Care of Business

That said, many boomer women who had children later in life are also now members of the so-called "sandwich generation," responsible for caring for kids as well as their aging parents. Nonprofit organizations and political campaigns that acknowledge these responsibilities and stressors and offer solutions will get an open ear. Women with a full care-giving plate are also often on the lookout for useful and concise information to help make their lives—and the decisions they have to make—easier.

4. Women of Color

The year 2006 was a milestone year for the nation's emerging majority. Nationally, people of color topped 100 million for the first time, which means they now make up a third of the population. According to Census Bureau projections, by 2050, half the nation's population will be comprised of people of color—African Americans, Latinos, Asian Americans, and Native Americans.

This demographic sea change is already being felt across America. Census data show that Whites are now the minority in nearly one in 10 of the nation's more than 3,000 counties, largely as the result of higher birth rates among African Americans and Hispanics and an immigrant influx, particularly from Central and South America. Seventy-one percent of Los Angeles County's population, or 7 million residents, are people of color, making it the county with the largest "minority" population in the country. According to the Selig Center for Economic Growth, African, Latino, and Asian Americans flexed their consumer muscle by spending *$1.6 trillion* in 2003—nearly triple what was spent in 1990. All of which is to say, the emerging majority will be increasingly important target audiences now and into the future for all sectors, business, nonprofit, and political.

"From a self preservation standpoint, you have to realize these communities are going to be more important"—to the economy and future of the country as a whole, according to Irasema Garza, director of external relations for Working America, an affiliate of the AFL-CIO, which organizes and advocates on behalf of working class Americans who do not belong to a union.

According to Garza, Corporate America has "long figured out that they need to expand their footprint in communities of color for their bottom line." Progressive organizations, she added, "can borrow a page from their playbook."

The minority vote is probably the single strongest element of the progressive coalition, according to political analyst Ruy Teixeira, a joint fellow at the Center for American Progress and The Century Foundation and co-author with John Judis of the book, *The Emerging Democratic Majority*. In the 2004 election, Black voters favored Kerry by 88–11 percent margin; Kerry had a 58–40 margin among Hispanics and a 56–44 among Asian Americans.

From a giving standpoint, polls show that, while most Americans believe that Whites give a greater percentage of their income to charities than minorities, Black women are more likely to give to charity than White women (in households with incomes of $25,000 or more), and they are more likely to give in excess of a thousand dollars. What's more, people of color are more likely to give when asked for a donation, but are asked less often than their White counterparts.

This last point is especially important given that marketing experts have observed that minority consumers tend to be loyal once they've made a brand selection. This is attributed in part to the fact that their interests have been historically neglected, so when one company addresses their needs directly, it can leave a lasting impression. What works for companies can work for cause campaigns and nonprofits, too.

Multicultural marketing is an entire industry unto itself, and it is beyond the scope of this book to go into significant detail into the many cultural signifiers, differences, acculturation levels, language abilities, and differences that set each ethnic group apart from Whites, from each other, as well as the differences within each group.

On the next page is a table of a few "fast facts" about the three largest ethnic groups in America.

African American	Latina	Asian American
1 in 4 women belong to a church	Median age is 26 compared to 30 for general female population	Fastest growing minority in the country
Women: Less likely to be married, greater financial responsibility	More likely to live in multigenerational homes	Majority are foreign-born: only 36% born in US
Value family, respect, diversity	Value family, hospitality, celebrations	Value family, education, respect for elders
2/3rds of women handle household financial planning and budgeting	Women exert important influence over family decisions—from purchases to voting	Highest median household income of any group, including Whites
Spend more time listening to radio	49% who watch television during prime-time hours watch Spanish-language programming	70% are online daily; more likely to get news, political info, and make purchases online than any other ethnic group
More likely to notice outdoor advertising (at bus stops, etc.) compared to other ethnic groups	3.5 times more likely to respond to a direct mail solicitation than other ethnic groups	78% consume both ethnic and English-language media, with print ranking above radio and TV

Below are some general principles to keep in mind when doing outreach to women of color:

Be Mindful of Cultural Differences

When NARAL Pro-Choice New York decided to take ownership of a public education campaign about "morning after" emergency contraceptives that originated with a group called the Reproductive Health Technologies Project, the organization knew Latinas had to be a prime audience because of the high rate of unintended pregnancy in the Latino community. But for the "Back Up Your Birth Control" campaign to fly among Latinas, its mascot, Rosie the Riveter, had to go.

The campaign was originally launched on college campuses for a young female audience that was highly educated and generally informed, if not engaged, with the feminist movements and women's causes. Rosie, the famous World War II icon, resonated as an image of female liberation and empowerment, according to Destiny Lopez, who was then NARAL Pro-Choice NY's vice president of programs.

But Lopez realized right away that Rosie wasn't a natural fit for the broad Latina audience that NARAL wanted to reach beyond the ivory tower.

"Hispanics might not have even known who she was," explained Lopez, now executive director of ACCESS, an advocacy and service reproductive rights organization based in Oakland, California. "We have different icons like Dolores Huerta for feminism and liberation." At worst, Lopez said, Rosie might have been come off unintentionally "like a maid—or Aunt Jemima."

Use Competent—and Culturally Competent—Translators

Britney Spears reportedly sports a tattoo of Chinese characters she intended to say "mysterious," but instead translates to "strange." In other words, when using translators, do your due diligence to make sure you're hiring consummate professionals.

When Fenton was working to rebrand Planned Parenthood Los Angeles, we brainstormed a number of different taglines for the organization. One of the things we wanted to get across was the passion and dedication the staff put into their work and taking care of their clients. But passion, translated literally as *pacion* didn't quite have the same connotation in Spanish. It leaned too much toward the passion of bodice-busting Harlequin romances or *telenovelas*. It was nixed.

The Messenger is as Important as the Message (so is the right political education)

Ultimately, if reaching out to people of color is critical to your mission and goals, you will be more successful if you have skilled people of color leading your outreach. This is important for both language and cultural competency reasons.

"Any group is going to trust someone who looks like them. That's human nature," according to Garza. "If you don't know your audience well, it's difficult to deliver the message."

Funders are also increasingly looking for diversity on staff and boards and reflected in coalition building activities in ways that are substantive and not tokenized. At the end of the day, however, it's a person's political education that matters more than their skin color—although being a member of an ethnic minority accounts for a lot.

For example, the fact that the civil rights and social justice group Opportunity Agenda is led by people of color "makes a big difference for decisions we make about the kind of programs we engage in, the issues we want to elevate, and the voices we promote," said Phoebe Eng, a co-founder of the group and the director of its sister organization, Creative Counsel. "All of this is really determined by our experience, our upbringing, and our social and political education."

Use the Community as Resource

Many of the nonprofits we work with don't have the resources to conduct focus groups to test messages. But don't let that stop you from testing altogether. Consult community groups that are working your target demographic; if you're deeply invested in connecting with diverse communities, it pays to coalition-build for a host of other reasons.

"If there's a need in your community, there's probably other groups that are doing the work too that you may want to ally with if there's a common cause," said Lopez, who added that, if a group lends you their cultural expertise, be ready and willing to give something back in return. "Sometimes progressives and nonprofits don't take the time to really learn about the community on whose behalf they're advocating, and that's a mistake."

When in Doubt, Consult the Experts

Cultural fluency is not something you learn overnight, and even professionals who specialize in multicultural marketing will tell you that they sometimes need to do a truth check on their own assumptions.

When Garza, who is of Mexican descent, was working in New Mexico on a public education project targeting Latino families, she made sure to work closely with AFL-CIO affiliates on the ground. She also dropped in on the director of a cultural center at the University of New Mexico to bone up on the historical and cultural background of her target demographic.

She learned, for example, that because the region was settled by Spaniards, "Hispano" is the preferred local term. "That's the sort of thing

I want to make sure I am communicating in the appropriate way because at the end of the day, my goal is to reach them," Garza said.

Differences are a Strength, Not a Liability

Nonprofits can fall into a dangerous trap when they abide by the notion that solidarity across differences trumps the differences themselves. In fact, just the opposite is true. Only by acknowledging and exploring our differences can we truly begin to strengthen movement building.

Recently, Eng consulted with a network of women's groups to organize a theme for an upcoming conference that had the explicit aim of engaging women of color. Among the themes that emerged was "trust" and what it means in the workplace, for power and in the context of race relations. In other words, instead of falling back on the safe and traditional "strength in diversity" frame, the organizers chose to put forward something with the potential to make some people uncomfortable, but that genuinely warranted discussion: Is there, in fact, trust between ethnic groups within the social change community? If not, what are the tensions, and what can be done to address them?

"All these concepts were brave because they did not shy away from what could be perceived as potential landmines," Eng said. "When we pose our projects as questions as opposed to conclusions, then we end up with richer discussions and better solutions that affect all of us. One size doesn't fit all—and that's okay."

Engage—and Listen

If women in general feel they aren't being listened to as a target demographic, it is even truer for women of color, according to the nonprofit communicators we talked to and the market research we reviewed.

Women of color are often considered an afterthought or an add-on. People sometimes think they have done their due diligence in addressing diversity when they've made sure there's an "ethnic person" in a photo montage rather than giving further consideration to how an overall marketing or outreach effort will include—or exclude—emerging majorities. The pay-off from doing it right can be considerable in terms of strengthening your outreach and your relevance to communities of color.

Just as we've discussed with single women, a demographic that has yet to be fully tapped, women of color are hungry for information and eager for an opening to engage, but they can feel ignored, invisible, and excluded from the conversation. The general principles for effective marketing apply to them, too. Show them you're paying attention. Ask them for their opinions. Draw out the issues and values that matter to them. Practice the outreach tactics that will connect with them. The results will pay off.

Conclusion

Women are a large and complex demographic. To market to them well takes an investment in educating yourself about where to reach them and how to engage them. While there are similarities in preferences and outlook for women in general, there are also important distinctions to be aware of if your goal is to connect with particular segments, whether generational or ethnic. Grounding yourself in research and working with professionals who know the lay of the land is worth the investment.

Chapter Take-Aways

- Not all women are the same. When reaching out to women, good social change marketers will consider their different and intersecting identities.

- Transitions in women's lives are excellent opportunities to meet women where they're at—college, marriage, motherhood, retirement, or empty nesting.

- Understanding your female demographic is critical to motivating her for action. Key tips for target groups include:

  — Single Women
    - Speak to financial security concerns.
    - Acknowledge her strength and independence vs. vulnerability.
    - Evoke opportunity.
    - Don't fall into the *Sex and the City* trap by thinking that all single women look, act, and think like Carrie Bradshaw.

continues

continued

—Mothers

- Value relationships, because she does.
- Save her time.
- Motivate her by invoking her power, not her guilt.
- When appropriate, don't overdo the "mom thing."
- Connect with her through her kids.

—Boomer Women

- Create "communal" opportunities.
- Acknowledge that she might be in a "sandwiched" care-giving situation.
- Give her useful and concise information.
- Provide "personal growth" activities connected to your mission.

—Women of Color

- Be mindful of cultural differences.
- Use competent—and culturally competent—translators.
- The messenger is as important as the message.
- Use the community as resource.
- When in doubt, consult the experts.

Engage—and listen.

Conclusion

The Not-So-Secret Secret to Changing the World

"Add Women and Change Everything."

In this book we've attempted to make the case that women are the biggest and most underutilized resource for social change by describing how critical they are for strengthening the forces that give rise to that change—advocacy, fundraising, electoral politics, and volunteering.

Women historically have been part of building democracy, according to Marie Wilson, the president of The White House Project, a nonprofit organization that promotes women's leadership. "We can't have a fully functioning society without engaging women." Her organization's tagline says it all: "Add women and change everything."

The trick to bringing women on board, however, is that it isn't a trick. Corporate marketers made the early mistake of painting products pink and thinking their job was done. Not so. Since then, a number of companies have taken a more sophisticated approach by first making a greater effort to understand women's concerns, needs, and aspirations. We've shown how the core principles behind this approach—caring, connecting, and community—can be harnessed by the public sector to make social change. Many nonprofits and progressive advocates are already applying these principles, however consciously or unconsciously. Our goal is to unleash even greater potential for social reform by encouraging progressives to market to women with more intent and purpose.

In this conclusion, we explore the greater ramifications of what it would mean if we were to market the value of community as a means for engendering social transformation on a global scale. If we did so, what would our world look like?

From Issues to Values

After John's Kerry's loss in the 2004 presidential election, a number of Democrats experienced a "come to Jesus" moment. We wouldn't be the first to critique the party or the larger progressive movement for focusing too narrowly on the "issues" and for failing to offer a broad and compelling vision anchored by the values that so many Americans hold dear. The value of serving a greater purpose beyond self-interest. The value of attending to the vulnerable and helpless. The value of affording everyone a shot at the American dream.

This book has been about nothing if not values. We would argue that, at the dawn of the 21st century, the social and political tides that define where and who we are as a people today make the values that matter most to women—connecting and community—a winning blueprint for social change and transformation.

The effects of globalization, terrorism, and the War in Iraq have made us more attuned to the need for cooperation and diplomacy. The vicious partisan infighting and deadlock that have come to define lawmaking in the nation's capital (and duplicated in legislatures across the country) have become untenable, given the urgency of the problems that face us. As progressives, we lose our way when we allow ourselves to devolve into masters of disaster when we should be lighting the way with hope. Meanwhile, conservatives have long figured out that political victory is achieved by waging culture wars. This is because values, not issues, ultimately win the loyalty of supporters—and voters.

We require a new progressive ethos for our time, one that goes beyond how we define our political stripes to one that defines our very lifestyles, imbedding itself into the very fiber of how we live our lives as card-carrying members of the human race. It's women who can lead the way.

Survival of the Connected

In his book, *A Darwinian Left: Politics, Evolution and Cooperation*, bioethicist Peter Singer describes how the modern-day theory of Social Darwinism, in which the ethics of the mighty conquering the weak is justified, was in fact constructed by early 20th century capitalists like Andrew Carnegie and John D. Rockefeller Jr., who were, at the time, waging a legal battle to prevent government from regulating industry.

"The growth of a large business is merely a survival of the fittest," according to Rockefeller, who described the ruling class' inevitable dominance over the laboring masses as "merely the working out of a law of nature and a law of God."

By placing this spin on Darwin's evolutionary theory squarely in its socio-political context, Singer reminds us that such theories are made, not born. For progressives seeking to reshape society, we need a "Darwinian left" that does not side-step the hard truths of human nature: namely, the hard-wiring that compels us to act in our own self-interest. In other words, if we appeal to the common good, we must be careful that we're not promoting a naïve and oversimplistic *Kumbaya* vision of togetherness.

But we know this, too, about human nature: money alone does not buy happiness, which is why the pursuit of wealth cannot be said to be the full or sole expression of self-interest. Human beings are also acting in their self-interest when they seek personal fulfillment and meaning in their lives.

As we have argued throughout this book, for many people, this meaning is found in community and in refuge from social and spiritual isolation. We're living in an age when families seldom sit together at the dinner table; when economic mobility has translated to social exile in the exurbs; and when the institutions that used to bring people together and anchor communities are floundering. The result is a palpable hunger among Americans for community, to be part of something bigger than themselves. Now more than ever, we need an ethos based on community. We call it "Survival of the Connected."

We need this sense of community in our politics, too. Like it or not, the biggest crises that now confront us, global warming and terrorism, all but ensure that (1) we cannot afford to "go it alone" or create adversaries and (2) cooperation is our greatest currency if we are to survive as a species. Indeed, we are less likely to "defect" and be driven solely by short-term benefits if we transform the rules of the game by truly stepping up and owning the fact that we are connected by a shared fate and a shared future. Nowhere is this more true than in the case of the global climate crisis, which will require all the nations of the world to do their parts to drive down carbon pollution and prevent the planet's literal meltdown. In the case of terrorism, is there any doubt, especially in light of recent history, that multilateralism is the only viable solution for protecting peace?

Changes in our political landscape, in our global economy, and in our social values—all of these must come into play as progressives re-envision reforms for the future. One thing that has not changed, however, is the primacy of community as the catalyst for transcendence. We may have to remake our houses, either by radically infusing old institutions with new energy, or starting new ones from scratch. But community—people uniting behind a common purpose—remains the source of strength, the genesis for big ideas capable of transforming society, and the vessel that contains our need to belong and to be part of a larger purpose.

The Death of Women's Issues?

In 2004, Michael Shellenberger and Ted Nordhaus unleashed a firestorm of controversy when they released a provocative article called "The Death of Environmentalism" that critiqued the policies and politics of modern environmentalism as inadequate for dealing with the crises of the day. They questioned whether the category of the "environment" even made sense, given that the framework of an Edenic nature that somehow exists apart from humankind seemed no longer useful, if it ever was.

In turn, a book about what matters to women and how to market must also interrogate the usefulness of "women's issues" as a political and social construction. We are not the first to pose the question, of course. We are at a time when other major social movements of the 20th century, from civil rights to labor, find themselves on a similar crossroads about their function and future.

So-called women's issues came of age with the first and second wave of feminists, who as "early adopters," had to fight to stake their claim in a world that did not recognize their role or their rights. By necessity, these earlier waves were preoccupied with securing these rights through legal and legislative means. Thanks in large part to these victories, times have changed, and so have the generations of women that followed.

"Young women have a different relationship to power—they assumed they should have it and don't think they should have to ask for it," said Wilson. The privileging and insistence on "equal rights" has become too limiting for younger women for whom these rights can be taken more or less for granted, and who are, as a consequence, more inclined to see their concerns and issues in a broader context beyond gender lines. This evolution is not limited to their perceptions, Wilson added. Issues traditionally thought of as "soft women's issues," such as health care, child care, education, are "now the hard security issues that are key to the sustainability of companies and our country."

Which is not to say that the category of "women's issues" is off life-support by any means, nor should it be.

Vivien Labaton, co-founder of the Third Wave Foundation and author of *The Fire This Time: Young Activists and the New Feminism,* was influential in our thinking on this matter. According to Labaton, "The fact of the matter is we still live in a world that suffers from sexism and inequality based on gender. To pretend that that's not the case gets you nowhere."

Just as we are not a color-blind society, we are not a gender equal society—nor should we be. We would argue that, rather than pretend that these inequalities and differences don't exist, we would do better to have them out in the open where they can be part of the conversation and part of the toolbox for shaping the society we want. Along those lines, there will be times when it is politically wise to mainstream women's issues and lose the labels, and times when it is not. There is no one fast and hard rule. Yet the progressive movement needs to feel some degree of pressure to make the priorities of women their own, just as it is incumbent upon the women's movement to frame and market their issues so that broader segments of the population make women's issues *their* issues.

An important part of this work involves switching from a needs-based to an assets-based positioning of women's role in society and how their contributions can improve community, nation, and the world. It means resisting the pigeon-holing of feminism as "choice only" and unearthing and marketing the deeper values—self-determination, community, caring, and fairness—that actually define it. If the women's movement is to stay relevant and healthy, it means women have to wage change equally on two fronts—the legal front as well as the cultural front because social transformation won't be achieved by incremental wins on the Hill or in the courts alone.

It's not only the women's movement that could benefit from a cultural shift. On a much broader scale, if we market effectively to women by drawing out what they value and respond to, we will be selling, so to speak, a lifestyle of caring and community that could help transform society from one of Survival of the Fittest to Survival of the Connected. Successful companies like Harley Davidson and Apple do much more than sell motorcycles, personal computers, and handheld devices. They sell an entire lifestyle that speaks to the dreams and aspirations of their customers.

Cultural transformation doesn't happen overnight, of course. But it can happen. Public perception—and acceptance—of gays and lesbians, for example, has shifted in recent years (although same-sex marriage remains a sticking point). There is no question that pop cultural phenomena like *Will & Grace* and *Queer Eye for the Straight Guy* helped introduce LGBT (lesbian, gay, bisexual, and transgender) people into American homes, and that savvy public education campaigns by groups like GLADD and Human Rights Campaign were instrumental in moving the needle by actively marketing the change they want to see the world embrace. Good marketing can influence how you live, not just what you buy.

Women: The Not-So-Secret Secret to Changing the World

Women get it. And they get it done. The question is: are we ready to listen to what they have to say and to unleash the knowledge, power, and potential they possess to make the world a better place? If the answer is yes, then the first step is to invest in education and, in some cases, reeducation. As Marti Barletta noted, even though both the theories behind and strategies for marketing to women have largely penetrated the corporate sector, they still meet with resistance and have yet to become the norm.

The reasons for this resistance are three-fold. One, old habits die hard, especially when we're not aware that we're doing anything wrong in the first place. In our view, marketing and communications campaigns positioned as gender-neutral are, in fact, often geared to what works for men, at the expense of what will appeal to and capture women's support. And what works for men—a global warming campaign, for example, that is long on facts about melting polar ice caps but short on how the problem will affect women's lives and doesn't include some indication of the steps they can take to protect their future—is missing opportunities to connect with women and what they care about.

Two, it requires rewiring decades of impassioned and ingrained polemics that subsumed gender *differences* in the interest of establishing gender *equality*. This can be tough for the majority of marketing executives in the boardroom, most of whom are from the generation of baby boomers who pioneered, and were the first to adopt, the principles of gender equality in the workplace and in the home.

Three is the concern that marketing to women will result in losing the attention and support of men. If you think back on the values and principles that matter to women—caring, connecting, and community—these are all things that we desire as human beings, male and female alike. But for women, they matter even more, which means if you can appeal to their threshold, you will sweep up men in the process. Remember, too, that women are "tougher customers"—they have a longer list of criteria that must be met before they're willing to green-light a decision. Generally speaking, this means if men cite defense and national security as their top political priorities, women care about these, too, along with their longer list of other priorities including healthcare, education, child care, and so on.

Putting Theory into Action

We hope this book has inspired you to rethink the way you carry out your marketing. We also hope you'll take these ideas to heart by applying them directly in your outreach to constituents. Here are five concrete ways to do it:

1. Ditch the niche.

If there's one thing we hope you'll take away from this book, it's to do away with the notion that women are a niche audience. As we've shown, women are the single most important audience you need to reach if you're in the business of making the world a better place because they make ideal donors, voters, and activists for your cause.

2. Be a "she spotter" and use the four Cs.

Now that you've ditched the niche, the next thing to do is run your marketing strategies and tactics through the filter of the things that resonate with women—the four Cs: care, connect, cultivate, and control.

Next time you launch a fundraising drive, a social marketing campaign, or an advocacy push, think creatively about ways that you can shape these efforts so they appeal to women's sensibilities.

3. Work in coalition.

Building community isn't just an effective strategy for mobilizing your constituents—it's also effective among nonprofit organizations for strengthening and marshalling their forces to achieve shared goals. When nonprofit groups join forces, the public sector becomes a formidable force. Many nonprofit organizations do this already, particularly when facing a common opponent, but coalition-building must become convention, especially given the enormity of the challenges confronting our world today. We've also heard repeatedly from program officers and other foundation staff that they want to fund more coalition-driven initiatives so efforts are not duplicated and their investment is multiplied.

4. Put your money where your mouth is.

This book has been largely written for public sector professionals, but there is a message for individual women, too. We've all been in conversations and gripe sessions where we air our frustrations, our grief, and our general dissatisfaction with the direction our country, or the world, is going. But if we are truly committed to shaking things up, we have to be willing to open our wallets and invest directly in the change we want to see in the world. This is not an easy thing for many women (including the authors!) who have spent a lifetime saving money in preparation for future and unknown calamities. But the social and environmental problems we face as a society are known all too well, and if we want to see change in our lifetime, we must be prepared to spend money in our lifetime to secure a better future for all of us. To put our money where our mouth is, we pledge 20% of the profits from this book to two of our favorite nonprofit organizations, Women for Women International and MomsRising.org.

5. Be part of a giving circle.

Of the many ideas and initiatives we discussed through the course of this book, the giving circle stands out as exemplary of the type of meaningful action we can all take, no matter how much or how little we make. For the public sector, this means encouraging and participating in these types of community-based philanthropic ventures that may fall outside traditional fundraising. For the individual, this means joining forces with like-minded people and educating yourself about the issues you care about, the organizations doing amazing work, and maximizing your philanthropy through the power of many, not one.

Creating progressive change will take much more than the right message, the right marketing, or the right issue. But it can begin by listening to and engaging the right people: women. The secret to changing the world is hidden in plain sight. If we recognize that women are not a niche audience but *the* audience and market to them effectively, we can unleash their transformative power to win health care for all, stop the climate crisis, achieve livable wages for working families, attain quality education for children, reduce domestic violence, and much more. This power will help people transition from the ethos of Survival of the Fittest to Survival of the Connected, because the global problems of the here and now and in our immediate future are problems that connect us all. The solutions, too, will be found in these connections, and in our responsibility to each other and to the planet. As we write this next chapter in our social evolution, we would be smart to enlist women as both our co-author and our muse.

Resources

Nonprofit Organizations:

AARP, www.aarp.org

American Lung Association, www.lungusa.org

American Society for the Prevention of Cruelty to Animals, www.aspca.org

BlogHer, www.BlogHer.org

Blue Shield of California Foundation, www.blueshieldcafoundation.org

CARE, www.care.org

Climate Counts, www.climatecounts.org

CODE PINK, www.codepink4peace.org

Corporate Accountability International, www.stopcorporateabuse.com

Current TV, www.current.com

EMILY'S List, www.emilyslist.org

Environmental Defense, www.environmentaldefense.org

Evangelical Environmental Network, www.creationcare.org

The Forum of Regional Grantmakers, www.givingforum.org

GLADD, www.gladd.org

Global Fund for Women, www.globalfundforwomen.org

Global Voices, www.globalvoicesonline.org

Go Ask Alice!, www.goaskalice.columbia.edu

Goldman Environmental Prize, www.goldmanprize.org

Heifer International, www.heifer.org

Human Rights Campaign, www.hrc.org

Independent Sector, www.independentsector.org

Innocence Project, www.innocenceproject.org

International Women's Media Foundation, www.iwmf.org

MomsRising, www.MomsRising.org

The Motherhood, www.themotherhood.net

MoveOn.org, www.moveon.org

NARAL Pro-Choice New York, www.prochoiceny.org

National Public Radio, www.npr.org

New York Asian Women's Shelter, www.nyawc.org

NRDC, www.nrdc.org

Opportunity Agenda, www.opportunityagenda.org

PETA, www.PETA.org

Pew Internet and American Life Project, www.pewinternet.org

The Pew Research Center for the People and the Press, www.people-press.org

Planned Parenthood Los Angeles, www.plannedparenthood.org/los-angeles

Ploughshares Fund, www.ploughshares.org

Project for Excellence in Journalism, www.journalism.org

Project KidSmart, www.projectkidsmart.org

Prostate Cancer Foundation, www.prostatecancerfoundation.org

Room to Read, www.roomtoread.org

Save the Children, www.savethechildren.org

Service Employees International Union (SEIU), www.seiu.org

Susan B. Komen Foundation, www.komen.org

Third Wave Foundation, www.thirdwavefoundation.org

UNICEF USA, www.unicefusa.org

VolunteerMatch, www.volunteermatch.org

The White House Project, www.thewhitehouseproject.org

Women Donors Network, www.womendonors.org

Women for Women International, www.womenforwomen.org

Women's Campaign Forum, www.wfconline.org

Women's Funding Network, www.wfnet.org

Women's Media Center, www.womensmediacenter.org

Women's Voices. Women Vote., www.wvwv.org

Working America, www.workingamerica.org

World Vision, www.worldvision.org

Books and Web Sites:

Marketing to Women Resources

Maria Bailey, *Trillion Dollar Moms: Marketing to A New Generation of Mothers* (New York, Kaplan Publishing, 2005)

Marti Barletta, *PrimeTime Women: How to Win the Hearts, Minds, and Business of Boomer Big Spenders* (Kaplan Publishing, 2007)

Marti Barletta, *Marketing to Women: How to Understand, Reach, and Increase Your Share of the World's Largest Market Segment* (AMACOM, 2003)

Mary Brown and Carol Orsborn, Ph.D., *BOOM: Marketing to the Ultimate Power Consumer—The Baby-Boomer Woman* (AMACOM, 2006)

Yvonne Divita, *Dickless Marketing: Smart Marketing to Women Online* (WME Books, 2004)

Lisa Johnson, *Mind Your X's and Y's: Satisfying the 10 Cravings of a New Generation of Consumers* (Free Press, 2006)

Lisa Johnson and Andrea Learned, *Don't Think Pink: What Really Makes Women Buy—and How to Increase Your Share of This Crucial Market* (AMACOM, 2003)

Tom Peters and Martha Barletta,*Trends* (DK Publishing, 2005)

Nonprofit and General Marketing and Fundraising Resources

Katya Andresen, *Robin Hood Marketing: Stealing Corporate Savvy to Sell Just Causes* (John Wiley & Sons, 2006)

Andy Goodman, http://www.agoodmanonline.com/purple.html

Chip Heath and Dan Heath, *Made to Stick: Why Some Ideas Survive and Others Die* (Random House Publishing Group, 2007)

Sondra C. Shaw and Martha A. Taylor, *Reinventing Fundraising: Realizing the Potential of Women's Philanthropy* (John Wiley & Sons, 1995)

Brain Science and Linguistics

Louann Brizendine, M.D., *The Female Brain* (Broadway Books, 2007)

George Lakoff, *Don't Think of an Elephant: Know Your Values and Frame the Debate—The Essential Guide for Progressives* (Chelsea Green Publishing, 2004) and *Moral Politics: How Liberals and Conservatives Think* (University of Chicago Press, 2002)

Deborah Tannen, Ph.D., *You Just Don't Understand: Women and Men in Conversation* (HarperCollins Publishers, 2007)

Progressive Resources

Kellyanne Conway, Celinda Lake, and Catherine Whitney, *What Women Really Want: How American Women Are Quietly Erasing Political, Racial, Class, and Religious Lines to Change the Way We Live* (Simon and Schuster Adult Publishing Group, 2005)

Laura Dawn, *It Takes a Nation: How Strangers Became a Family in the Wake of Hurricane Katrina* (Mandala Publishing, 2006)

Allison Fine, *Momentum: Igniting Social Change in the Connected Age* (John Wiley & Sons, 2006)

Peter Singer, *A Darwinian Left: Politics, Evolution, and Cooperation* (Yale University Press, 2000)

Women's Campaign Forum Foundation, *Vote with Your Purse: Harnessing the Power of Women's Political Giving for the 2008 Elections and Beyond* (2007), http://www.wcfonline.org/uploads/WCFF%20Vote%20w_Purse%20Report.pdf

All this information (and more) is available at www.SheSpotBook.com.

Notes

Introduction Notes

2   "83 percent of all consumer purchases," Marti Barletta, "Big Economic Opportunity in Marketing to Women," *Advertising Age*, April 2, 2007, http://adage.com/point/article?article_id=115892

2   "health care-related decisions for their households," U.S. Department of Labor, General Facts on Women and Job Based Health, http://www.dol.gov/ebsa/newsroom/fshlth5.html (accessed December 2, 2007).

2   "women are where the money is," Tom Peters and Martha Barletta, *Trends* (New York, DK Publishing, Inc., 2005), p. 13.

2   "socially conscious investors," Steve Schueth, "Socially Responsible Investing in the U.S.," *Journal of Business Ethics*, Volume 43, Number 3 / March, 2003, p. 189–194.

3   "32 percent of women volunteer," "Women Volunteer at Higher Rates than Men Across US, New Federal Study Finds," Press Release, Corporation for National and Community Service, June 13, 2006.

Chapter 1 Notes

12   "single women outnumber married ones," Sam Roberts, "51% of Women Are Now Living Without Spouse," *New York Times*, Jan 16, 2007.

13   "women continue to earn 78 cents," US Bureau of Labor Statistics, "Highlights of Women's Earnings in 2002," September 2003, http://www.bls.gov/cps/cpswom2002.pdf

13   "women control slightly more than half," A Pivotal Role, Wealth, Financial & Lifestyle Perspective from Northern Trust, Winter 2007, Northern Trust, 17 May 2007, http://www .northerntrust.com/wealth/07-winter/apivotalrole.html (based on information from the Federal Reserve Bank), Michael J. Silverstein, Senior Partner and Managing Director, The Boston Consulting Group, Personal Interview, May 27, 2007.

13   "83 percent of all household purchases," Tom Peters and Martha Bar-letta, *Trends* (New York, DK Publishing, Inc., 2005), p. 32–33.

13   "3.3 trillion in purchasing power," Advancingwomen.com, "Women Business Owners—World's Fastest Growing Market," http://64.233.169.104/search?q=cache:wxgpus0fakMJ:www.witi. com/center/aboutwiti/press/downloads/women_fast_growing_mar-ket.pdf+Women-owned+businesses+today+are+the+fastest-growing +sector+of+the+U.S.+economy,+representing+%243.3+trillion+in+pur chasing+power.&hl=en&ct=clnk&cd=1&gl=us

13   "growing at six times the rate of all US firms," Businesses Owned by Women of Color in the United States, Center for Women's Business Research, 2004.

13   "more likely than men to graduate," Claudia Buchmann and Thomas A. DiPrete, "The Growing Female Advantage in College Completion: The Role of Family Background and Academic Achievement," *American Sociological Review*, Vol. 71, No. 4, August 2006; and Claudia Buch-mann and Thomas A. DiPrete, "Gender-Specific Trends in the Value of Education and the Emerging Gender Gap in College Completion," *Demography*—Vol. 43, Number 1, February 2006.

14   "prime target for fundraising," Mary Lou Quinlan, *Just Ask a Women, Cracking the Code of What Women Want and How They Buy* (New York, John Wiley and Sons), p. 60.

14   "take greater risks," "*Women make twice as many charitable contributions as men do,*" Women and Philanthropy: Understanding and Engaging a High Potential Audience (n.d.) Council of Michigan Foundations April 13, 2007 (citing B.W. Johnson and J.P. Rosenfeld, "Examining the factors that Affect Charitable Giving," Trusts and Estates, 1991, p. 30).

14   "more than half donate $25,000," National Foundation for Women Business Owners, "Business Women of Achievement Are Independent Philanthropists: Members of Women's Business Group Are Substantial Givers," Press Release, November 12, 1999, http://www.nfwbo.org

14   "more likely to contribute at least $10,000," "Survey Finds Business Owners Are Philanthropic Leaders," Press Release, November 14, 2000, http://www.cfwbr.org

15   "sea change in political leadership," Christy Hoppe, "Election '08: Campaign boosted by 'unprecedented' trend," *Dallas Morning News*, Oct. 28, 2007.

15   "causes they believe will bring about social change," Sondra C. Shaw and Martha Taylor, *Reinventing Fundraising: Realizing the Potential of Women's Philanthropy* (San Francisco: Jossey-Bass, 1995), p. 88-89.

15   "70 percent of program officer positions," Elizabeth Randolph, "Women Give More than Ever Yet Get Small Returns," Women's ENews, December 21, 2000, http://www.womensenews.org/article. cfm/dyn/aid/380/context/archive

16   "Senator Jim Webb's victory" Ms. Magazine and Women Donors Network, "Women Voters Made the Difference in the 2006 Election," November 17, 2006, http://msmagazine.com/radar/2006-11-17-poll-results.pdf

17   "30 year high in volunteering," Stephanie Boraas White, "Volunteer-ing in the United States 2005," Bureau of Labor Statistics, http://www. bls.gov/opub/mlr/2006/02/ressum.pdf

17   "profile of the typical American volunteer," "Women Volunteer at Higher Rates than Men Across US, New Federal Study Finds," Press Release, Corporation for National and Community Service June 13, 2006.

17   "more likely to volunteer," Ibid.

18   "volunteers are critical for success," Mark. A Hager, "Volunteer Man-agement Capacity in America's Charities and Congregations," The Ur-ban Institute, March 2004, http://www.urban.org/url.cfm?ID=410963

18   "claim responsibility for providing bulk of that pot," Independent Sector (2006) The estimated dollar value of volunteer time is $18.77 per hour for 2005. (Washington, DC: author) Retrieved June 1, 2006 from http://www.independentsector.org/programs/research/volun-teer_time.html

18 "how to make smart choices," Columbia University Graduate School of Journalism's Alumni Association Lecture series "What Women Want: Media, Myth and Reality." November 28, 2006.

18 "men like service," Ibid.

Chapter 2 Notes

25 "full understanding of the scope," Anne Moir and David Jessel, *Brain Sex: The Real Difference Between Men and Women* (Dell Publishing, 1991), p. 168–170.

25 "a contest to preserve independence," Deborah Tannen, *You Just Don't Understand* (New York, HarperCollins Publishers, 2007), p. 24–25.

26 "girl's play...boy's play," Louann Brizendine and Susan Wells, *The Female Brain* (New York, Morgan Road Books, 2006), p. 24.

Chapter 3 Notes

32 "the force that creates relationships," Anne Moir and David Jessel, *Brain Sex: The Real Difference Between Men and Women* (Dell Publishing, 1991), p. 129.

32 "questions women raised," Ibid., p. 169.

33 "kind of personI would most like to be," Ibid., p.129.

34 "43 percent of women voters reported attending religious services," Kellyanne Conway, Celinda Lake, and Catherine Whitney, *What Women Really Want: How American Women Are Quietly Erasing Political, Racial, Class and Religious Lines to Change the Way We Live* (Simon & Schuster Adult Publishing Group, October 2005), p. 211.

35 "shaking things up by changing the systems," Jo Gruidly Moore and Mariann Philbin, "Women as Donors: Old Stereotypes, New Visions," *Women, Philanthropy, and Social Change*, Elayne Clift, ed. (Medford, MA: Tufts University Press, 2005), p. 67, 71.

37 "a one time phenomenon," Mark Hugo Lopez, Emily Kirby, and Jared Sagoff, "Voter Turnout Among Young Women and Men: Fact Sheet," The Center for Information & Research on Civic Learning and Engagement, July 2005.

37 "80 percent of Americans say," Survey of 1,004 American adults commissioned by The White House Project and administered by Roper Public Affairs, September 2005.

37 "a strong position on national security," Survey of 1,000 registered likely voters commissioned by The White House Project and administered by Lake Research Partners, September 2006, http://www.thewhitehouseproject.org/culture/researchandpolls/security2006.php

38 "by giving to an organization I support," Sondra C. Shaw and Martha Taylor, *Reinventing Fundraising: Realizing the Potential of Women's Philanthropy* (San Francisco: Jossey-Bass, 1995), p. 86.

38 "desire to give in a more selfless way," Ibid., p. 85–86.

39 "women don't buy brands," Faith Popcorn and Lys Marigold, *EVEolution: The Eight Truths of Marketing to Women* (New York: Hyperion, 2000), p. 4.

40 "violations of women's rights," Carol Tarvis, *Mismeasure of Woman* (New York, Simon & Schuster Adult Publishing Group, 1993), p. 17.

40 "never a better time to be a woman," Kellyanne Conway, Celinda Lake, and Catherine Whitney, *What Women Really Want: How American Women Are Quietly Erasing Political, Racial, Class and Religious Lines to Change the Way We Live* (Simon & Schuster Adult Publishing Group, October 2005), p. 218.

41 "they want more time," New American Dream, "Americans Eager to Take Back Their Time: Over Half Would Trade a Days Pay for Less Work and Less Stress," August 2003, http://www.newdream.org/live/time/timepoll.php

Chapter 4 Notes

46 "huge amounts of estrogen," Louann Brizendine and Susan Wells, *The Female Brain* (New York, Morgan Road Books, 2006), p. 18–19.

46 "emotional mirroring...triggers are especially active," Ibid, p. 122.

47 "operative emotion is not envy," Marti Barletta, *Marketing to Women: How to Increase Your Share of the World's Largest Market Segment* (New York, Kaplan Publishing, 2006), p. 55.

53 "men want the headlines," Tom Peters and Martha Barletta, *Trends* (New York, DK Publishing, Inc., 2005), p. 92.

54 "demonstrating the success of individuals," Home Depot's True Stories: In Every Project there Is a True Story, www6.homedepot.com/truestories/index. html?cm_mmc=THD_MarketingTrueStoriesDigitas-TOH_PBS (no longer available).

55 "Health Department reported receiving 15,000 calls," "Anti-Smoking Ads Shock Viewers in NYC," *Good Morning America*, ABC News, June 15, 2006.

57 "concerned with conforming to social norms," Chip Health and Dan Heath, *Made to Stick: Why Some Ideas Survive and Others Die* (New York, Random House, 2006), p. 188–190.

60 "prefer that life be fair," Christopher Hitchens, "Why Women Aren't Funny," *Vanity Fair*, January 2007.

53 "impressive but somewhat detached," Mark Leibovich, "Polished and Upbeat, Romney Tries to Connect," *New York Times*, June 16, 2007.

Chapter 5 Notes

67 "invited viewers to determine the outcome," Lev Grossman, "Time's Person of the Year: You," December 13, 2006, http://www.time.com/ time/magazine/article/0,9171,1569514,00.html

70 "advertising that shows more women doing things together," Marti Barletta, *Marketing to Women: How to Increase Your Share of the World's Largest Market Segment* (New York, Kaplan Publishing, 2006), p. 214.

Chapter 6 Notes

78 "a deep well of support and involvement," Sondra C. Shaw and Martha Taylor, *Reinventing Fundraising: Realizing the Potential of Women's Philanthropy* (San Francisco: Jossey-Bass, 1995), p. 90.

79 "give to help others," Bonita Banducci, "Women's Philanthropic Leadership—How is it different?," p 43: R. Newman, cited in Hall, 2004, p.3, Wiley Interscience, http://www3.interscience.wiley.com/ cgi-bin/abstract/112580143/ABSTRACT?CRETRY=1&SRETRY=0

79 "92 percent said they relied on word of mouth," Marti Barletta, *Marketing to Women: How to Increase Your Share of the World's Largest Market Segment* (New York, Kaplan Publishing, 2006), p. 123.

79 "they'll build you a pipeline of referrals," Delia Passi and A.B. Aronson, *Winning the Toughest Customer: The Essential Guide to Selling to Women* (Kaplan 2006), p. 108.

79 "women had increased their giving by 22 percent," "Vote with Your Purse: Harnessing the Power of Women's Political Giving in 2008," Women's Campaign Forum Foundation, 2007 http://www.wcfonline. org/uploads/WCFF%20Vote%20w_Purse%20Report.pdf and interview with Ilana Goldman, President, Women's Campaign Forum Foundation.

80 "$41 to $136 trillion that is expected to transfer," "A Plan (of one's own)—New Ventures in Philanthropy," (Boston College Social Welfare Research Institute), October 20, 1990.

81 "women are more likely to open their pocketbooks," S.C. Shaw, D. Sublett, and M. Sommerfeld, cited in Hall, 2004, p. 3.

82 "ninety percent of the donations it receives," See example: http://www.savethechildren.org/about/financial.html.

84 "men are more prone to 'go it alone'," Delia Passi and A.B. Aronson, *Winning the Toughest Customer* (Kaplan Publishing 2006), p. 45.

84 "already made that organization jump," Marti Barletta, *Marketing to Women: How to Increase Your Share of the World's Largest Market Segment* (New York, Kaplan Publishing, 2006), p. 122–123.

85 "what ultimately drives purchase," Delia Passi and A.B. Aaronson, *Winning the Toughest Customer: The Essential Guide to Selling to Women* (New York, Kaplan Publishing, 2006), p. 30.

89 "where specifically they want their money to go," Julie Bick, "Write a Check? The New Philanthropist Goes Further," *New York Times*, March 18, 2007.

90 "a window onto the types of projects World Vision funds," http://wvus.blogspot.com/?cmp=ILC-blog#115706666193821651

90 "giving circles came about in the early 1990s," "More Giving Together: The Growth and Impact of Giving Circles and Shared Giving," Forum of Regional Associations of Grantmakers, 2006, http://www.givingforum.org/s_forum/bin.asp?CID=639&DID=5316&DOC=FILE.PDF

Chapter 7 Notes

98 "power to help her," see CARE's "I am Powerful" campaign visuals go to http://www.care.org/search/index.asp?cx=01414375215338110315 2%3Afuf_wt90flk&cof=FORID%3A11&q=i+am+powerful.&sa.x=0&sa.y=0&sa=Search

99 "we dreamed the change," see the film at: http://www.climatecounts.org/whatis.php

99 "reduce global warming pollution," see the score card at: http://www.climatecounts.org/pdf/ClimateCountsWalletCardBW607.pdf

102 "What kind of footprint will you leave?" http://www.timberland.com/timberlandserve/timberlandserve_index.jsp

102   "how much energy," http://www.timberland.com/corp/index. jsp?page=csr_resource_consumption

103   "It's not just words and information," Mickey Meese, "What Do Women Want? Just Ask." *New York Times*, Oct. 29, 2006.

103   "If she has to ask," Faith Popcorn and Lys Marigold, *EVEolution: The Eight Truths of Marketing to Women* (New York: Hyperion, 2000), p. 79.

104   "download the pocket guide," http://www.environmentaldefense. org/documents/1980_pocket_seafood_selector.pdf

Chapter 8 Notes

109   "probably the worst place to meet guys," "Single Minded—What's Going on In the Head of the Single New York Women," *Time Out New York*, June 28-July 4, 2007.

110   "the press is no longer a gatekeeper," Rick Edmonds, Andrew Tyndall, and Bill Kovach, "State of the News Media 2007, An Annual Report on American Journalism," *Project for Excellence In Journalism*, 2007, http://www.stateofthenewsmedia.com/2007/narrative_overview_in-tro.asp?media

110   "more likely to scan," RTO Online, "Why It's Difficult for Marketers to Reach Women 25–54; 62 Percent have Little Time for Commercial Messages," March 16, 2005, http://www.rtoonline.com/content/ar-ticle/Mar05/MarketingToWomen031605.asp

110   "given the 'king maker' effect," Ibid.

111   "people for whom she filters information," Ibid.

111   "part of a general rising trend," Rick Edmonds, Andrew Tyndall, and Bill Kovach, "State of the News Media 2007, An Annual Report on American Journalism," *Project for Excellence In Journalism*, 2007, http://www.stateofthenewsmedia.com/2007/narrative_overview_in-tro.asp?media

111   "66 percent of people who follow political news closely," Ibid.

111   "Television remains the most popular news source," Globe Scan, "BBC, Reuters and Media Center Poll: Trust in Media Poll—Me-dia More Trusted than the Governments," May 3, 2005, http:// www.globescan.com/news_archives/bbcreut_country.html and http://199.202.238.2/news_archives/Trust_in_Media.pdf

111   "a few years ago there was little or no gender gap," The Pew Research Center for People and the Press "New Audiences Increasingly Politi-cized, Online News Audience Larger and More Diverse," June 8, 2004. http://people-press.org/reports/display.php3? PageID=833

112 "Other new audio formats are more balanced," Arbitron, "Public Radio Today: How America Listens to Public Radio Stations," July 27, 2006 and "Radio Today: How Americans Listen to Radio, 2006 Edition," February 14, 2006.

112 "The news gender gap," The Pew Research Center for People and the Press, "Where Americans Go for News," 2004, http://people-press.org/reports/display.php3?PageID=834

112 "online news consumption has grown steadily," The Pew Research Center for People and the Press "New Audiences Increasingly Politicized, Online News Audience Larger and More Diverse," June 8, 2004. http://people-press.org/reports/display.php3? PageID=833

112 "paying attention to consumer trends," Rick Edmonds, Andrew Tyndall, and Bill Kovach, "State of the News Media 2007, An Annual Report on American Journalism," Project for Excellence In Journalism, 2007, http://www.stateofthenewsmedia.com/2007/narrative_overview_intro.asp?media

113 "Beyond email, they also use it as a platform," Gord Hotchkiss, "How Gender Affects Search, Part 2 Gord Hotchkiss," Media Post Publications, *Search Insider: The Inside Line on Search Marketing*, January 12, 2006, http://publications.mediapost.com/index.cfm?fuseaction=Articles.showArticle&art_aid=38407

113 "driving this sea change," Allison Fine, *Momentum, Igniting Social Change in a Connected Age* (Hoboken, John Wiley & Sons, 2006), p. 60.

113 "women preferred pages with more color," Michael Rubikam,"Sex differences matter on the Internet," Associated Press, August 10, 2005.

114 "important online marketing tips," Yvonne Divita, "Marketing to Women Online: How Women Use the Web," *Dickless Marketing*, http://www.marketingtowomenonline.com/.

116 "profiles of mother and daughter donors," To see example of the Global Fund for Women's donor support letter go to http://www.globalfundforwomen.org/cms/about-gfw/supporters/crisanta-de-guzman.html

117 "Tips From Our Road Warriors," Joe Sharkey, "Maybe a Lavender Web Site Wasn't How to Attract Women," *New York Times*, April 17, 2007.

117 "more women play online mobile games," "Telephia Reports One-Third of Mobile Game Revenues Driven by Puzzle/Strategy Games, with Tetris, Tetris Deluxe and Bejeweled Leading the Pack: Women Drive More Than Two-Thirds of Mobile Game Revenues", Nielsen Mobile, June 26, 2006. http://www.telephia.com/html/insights_062606.html

118 "more Americans are reading blogs," Amanda Lenhart and Susannah Fox, "Bloggers: A Portrait of the Internet's New Storytellers," July 19, 2006, Pew Internet and American Life Project, http://www.pewinternet.org/pdfs/PIP%20Bloggers%20Report%20July%2019%202006.pdf

118 "more likely than men to continue blogging," Maura Welch, "Women tap the power of the blog," *Boston Globe* July 17, 2006.

119 "when it comes to watching videos online," "How Women Look at Video Online is Different," *eMarketer*, March 27, 2007, http://www.emarketer.com/Article.aspx?id=1004705

119 "more likely to surf for entertainment," Ibid.

119 "56 percent of female students polled," Peter Burrows, "Another Perspective on Face Book", *BusinessWeek,* March 29, 2006, http://www.businessweek.com/the_thread/techbeat/archives/2006/03/another_perspec.html

119 "according to current traffic trends," ComScore Networks, "More than Half of MySpace Visitors are Now 35 or Older, As the Sites Demographic Composition Continues to Shift," October 5, 2006, http://www.comscore.com/press/release.asp? press=1019

120 "a handful of sites aimed specifically at moms," Rohit Bhargara, "Analysis: Six Useful Social Media Tools for Women," *DMW Daily*, June 26, 2007, http://www.dmwmedia.com/news/2007/06/26/analysis-6-useful-social-media-tools-and-sites-for-women

Chapter 9 Notes

122 "gave us a way of finding people," Yochi J. Dreazen, "Democrats, Playing Catch-Up, Tap Database to Woo Potential Voters," *Wall Street Journal*, Oct 31, 2006.

124 "in sync with a 60 year old," Stan Greenberg, Anna Greenberg, David Walker, "The Marriage Gap: Marital Status Crucial Dynamic in American Politics," Greenberg Quinlan Rosner and Page Gardner, Women's Voices. Women Vote, June 21, 2007. http://www.wvwvactionfund.org/docs/mgap.pdf

124 "according to an exit poll," Dennis Cauchon, "Marriage gap could sway elections," *USA Today*, Sept. 27, 2006.

124 "a 32 point gap in the 2006 election," Susan Page, "Married? Single? Status affects how women vote," *USA Today*, Aug. 25, 2004, and Stan Greenberg, Andrew Baumann, and Dave Walker, "A New America: Unmarrieds Drive Political and Social Change," Greenberg Quinlan

Rosner, November 1, 2007, http://www.greenbergresearch.com/articles/2092/3957_1031m10_FINAL.pdf

125 "married women have traditionally cast more ballots," Laurel Elder, Steven Greene "The Myth of "Security Moms" and "NASCAR Dads": Parenthood, Political Stereotypes, and the 2004 Election,"*Social Science Quarterly* 88 (1), 1–19. doi:10.1111/j.1540-6237.2007.00443 (2007).

126 "81 percent of women between the ages of 40 and 44," "Mothers by the Numbers" U.S. Census Bureau, 2007, http://www.infoplease.com/spot/momcensus1.html

126 "most powerful consumer in the U.S.," Maria Bailey and Bonnie W. Ulman, *Trillion Dollar Moms: Marketing to A New Generation of Mothers* (New York, Kaplan Publishing, 2005),
p. xi.

127 "mothers are significantly more liberal," L Elder and S. Greene, "The Politics of Parenthood, 1972–2004," Paper presented at the annual meeting of the American Political Science Association, Marriott, Loews Philadelphia, and the Pennsylvania Convention Center, Philadelphia, PA, August, 2006.

127 "the inkling of a new movement," Kara Jesella, "Mom's Mad. And She's Organized," *New York Times*, February 22, 2007.

128 "customers think in terms of related activities," Lisa Johnson and Andrea Learned, *Don't Think Pink* (AMACOM, 2003), p. 169.

129 "80 percent more likely to buy a product," Maria Bailey and Bonnie W. Ulman, *Trillion Dollar Moms: Marketing to A New Generation of Mothers* (New York, Kaplan Publishing, 2005).

131 "mothers truly had distinctive political preferences," Laurel Elder, Steven Greene (2007) "The Myth of "Security Moms" and "NASCAR Dads": Parenthood, Political Stereotypes, and the 2004 Election,"*Social Science Quarterly,* 88 (1), 1–19. doi:10.1111/j.1540-6237.2007.00443

133 "bringing like minded people together," Joanna L. Krotz, Microsoft Small Business Center ,"What do Boomers Want in 2006," *Imago Creative*, February 9, 2006, http://www.imagocreative.com/about/imago_news.php?NewsID=000034

133 "by 2050 half the nation's population," "Minorities Become the Majority in 10 Percent of U.S. Counties," Associated Press, August 9, 2007.

133 "Seventy-one percent of Los Angeles County's population," United

States Census Bureau, "More the 300 Counties Majority Minority," August 9, 2007 http://www.census.gov/Press-Release/www/releases/archives/population/010482.html

133 "flexed their consumer muscle," Jeffery M. Humphries, "The Multi-cultural Economy 2003: America's Minority Buying Power," Georgia Business and Economic Condition—University of Georgia, Second Quarter 2003. http://www.ethnicmajority.com/Attachments/Selig%20UGA%20report%20on%20minority%20buying%20power.pdf

134 "In the 2004 election," Ruy Teixeira, "The Minority Vote and the Progressive Coalition," *The Emerging Democratic Majority*, February 2, 2006, http://www.emergingdemocraticmajorityweblog.com/donkey-rising/archives/001375.php

134 "more likely to give when asked for a donation," "The Contemporary Charitable Giving and Voluntarism of Black Women," Paper presented at the Center for the Study of Philanthropy, City University of New York, Conference on Women and Philanthropy: Past, Present and Future, New York, NY, June 1987.

134 "What works for companies," "The New Majority Marketing to Minorities," http://www.sba.gov/gopher/Business-Development/Success-Series/Vol6/mktg.txt

134–135 "fast facts about the three largest ethnic groups," Laura Sonderup, "Hispanic Marketing: A Critical Market Segment," April 2004, http://www.ad-mkt-review.com/public_html/docs/fs075.html; Lisa Johnson and Andrea Learned, *Don't Think Pink* (AMACOM, 2003), p. 139–45; Debra Aho Williamson, "Marketing to African Americans Online," *iMedia Connection*, November 4, 2005, http://www.imediaconnection.com/content/7202.asp; "Study on Asian American Consumer Trends," November 2, 2005. http://www.aaja.org/news/community/2005_11_04_1/; Saul Gitlin, "The Asian-American Market: Midway Between Census 2000 and 2010." http://www.multicultural.com/experts/art_asian.html; and Tom Spooner, "Asian Americans and the Internet: the Young and Connected," Pew Internet & American Life Project, December 12, 2001.

Conclusion

143 "a law of nature and a law of God," Peter Singer, *A Darwinian Left: Politics, Evolution and Cooperation* (Yale University Press, 1999), p. 11.

Acknowledgments

The authors wish to thank:

Nick Allen, Donordigital

Medea Benjamin, CODE PINK

Joan Blades, MomsRising.org and co-founder of MoveOn.org

Kathy Bonk, Communications Consortium Media Center

Barbara Brenner, Breast Cancer Action

Julie Burton, women's advocate

Amanda Cooper, UNITE HERE!

Wendy Dembo, trend and strategic marketing consultant

Phoebe Eng, Opportunity Agenda

Allison Fine, author of *Momentum: Igniting Social Change in a Connected Age*

Page Gardner, Women's Voices. Women Vote.

Irasema Garza, Working America

Ilana Goldman, Women's Campaign Forum Foundation

Douglas Gould, Douglas Gould and Company

Chris Grumm, Women's Funding Network

Donna Hall, Women Donors Network

Arianna Huffington, author and founder, *The Huffington Post*

Vivien Labaton, co-editor of *The Fire This Time: Young Activists and New Feminism*

Celinda Lake, Lake Research Partners

George Lakoff, Rockridge Institute and author of *Don't Think of an Elephant* and *Moral Politics*

Destiny Lopez, ACCESS—Women's Health Rights Coalition

Holly Minch, Spitfire Strategies

Zainab Salbi, Women for Women International

Daniel Silverman, Irvine Foundation

Andrea Dew Steel, Emerge America, and Susie Tompkins Buell Foundation

Mal Warwick, Mal Warwick Associates

Marie Wilson, The White House Project

Naomi Wolf, author

We are in debt to their expertise and to their guidance for the fruitful directions their thoughts took us in the writing of this book.

Thanks go to Gary Hirshberg, CE-Yo of Stonyfield Yogurt for his thoughtful foreword.

We want to say a special thanks to these women for their pioneering work in the field of marketing to women:

Marti Barletta, The TrendSight Group

Yvonne Divita, Windsor Media Enterprises, LLC

Lisa Johnson, Reach Group Consulting

Andrea Learned, Learned on Women

Delia Passi, Medelia Communications

Faith Popcorn, BrainReserve

Thanks as well to Martha A. Taylor and Sondra Shaw-Hardy, co-authors of *Reinventing Fundraising: Realizing the Potential of Women's Philanthropy* for their scholarship on women in philanthropy.

Gratitude also to:

Morra Aarons-Mele

Curt Alexander

Nick Arons

Larae Booker and Merritt Fog, our book interns

Andrew Boyd

Gita Drury

Lauren Eskelin

Emily Evers

Wende Jager-Hyman and the Woodhull Institute

Carol Jenkins and the Women's Media Center

Anna Lappé

Alice Markowitz

Emily Mckhann

Katie Orenstein

Eli Pariser

Ricken Patel

Erica Payne

Sasha Post

Progress with Friends

Cathy Renna

Jason Scott Jones

Wood Turner

Johanna Vondeling, our editor

Elizabeth Wagley

Ricki Weisberg

Ben Wikler

Antha Williams

and Lisa W.'s husband Christoph Brem for his encouragement, brain waves, inspiration, and for holding baby Bruno so she could type.

Finally, a special shout-out to our colleagues and clients at Fenton Communications—with special thanks to Barrie Koegel, Matt Ipcar, Amanda Fox, Ashley Harness, Erica Sackin, Sarah Bacon, Liz London, Sam Boykin, David Fenton, and Arleen Troy.

Index

About the Authors

Lisa Witter

Lisa Witter is the chief operating officer of Fenton Communication, where she heads the firm's practice in women's issues and global affairs. Her clients include Women for Women International, Global Fund for Women, Women's Funding Network, MoveOn.org, William and Flora Hewlett Foundation, Harvard School of Public Health, and American Medical Association.

Co-founder of the award-winning SheSource.org, a database of women experts to help close the gender gap among commentators in the news media, Witter is a political and social commentator and blogger, who in 2004 was featured in Showtime's American Candidate. Honored as an outstanding activist and expert on women's issues by Oxygen.com for her work on a national campaign against privatizing Social Security during the 2000 presidential election, she is on the board of directors or advisory council for Climate Counts, MomsRising.org, and Women for Women International.

Lisa Chen

Lisa Chen, a former reporter with the San Jose Mercury News, has been working in the public interest communications field for the past 10 years, serving clients including the New York Academy of Medicine, National Urban League, Physicians for Human Rights, Blue Shield of California Foundation, EngenderHealth, and Asian Americans/Pacific Islanders in Philanthropy.

A senior vice president at Fenton Communications, she is the firm's head editor and writer and develops creative messaging for clients across a broad spectrum of issues, ranging from public health to education reform. Her writing has been published in the *New York Times, USA Today, Boston Globe, San Francisco Chronicle,* and elsewhere.

She lives in New York City.

About Berrett-Koehler Publishers

Berrett-Koehler is an independent publisher dedicated to an ambitious mission: Creating a World That Works for All.

We believe that to truly create a better world, action is needed at all levels—individual, organizational, and societal. At the individual level, our publications help people align their lives with their values and with their aspirations for a better world. At the organizational level, our publications promote progressive leadership and management practices, socially responsible approaches to business, and humane and effective organizations. At the societal level, our publications advance social and economic justice, shared prosperity, sustainability, and new solutions to national and global issues.

A major theme of our publications is "Opening Up New Space." They challenge conventional thinking, introduce new ideas, and foster positive change. Their common quest is changing the underlying beliefs, mindsets, institutions, and structures that keep generating the same cycles of problems, no matter who our leaders are or what improvement programs we adopt.

We strive to practice what we preach—to operate our publishing company in line with the ideas in our books. At the core of our approach is stewardship, which we define as a deep sense of responsibility to administer the company for the benefit of all of our "stakeholder" groups: authors, customers, employees, investors, service providers, and the communities and environment around us.

We are grateful to the thousands of readers, authors, and other friends of the company who consider themselves to be part of the "BK Community." We hope that you, too, will join us in our mission.

Be Connected

Visit Our Website

Go to www.bkconnection.com to read exclusive previews and excerpts of new books, find detailed information on all Berrett-Koehler titles and authors, browse subject-area libraries of books, and get special discounts.

Subscribe to Our Free E-Newsletter

Be the first to hear about new publications, special discount offers, exclusive articles, news about bestsellers, and more! Get on the list for our free e-newsletter by going to www.bkconnection.com.

Get Quantity Discounts

Berrett-Koehler books are available at quantity discounts for orders of ten or more copies. Please call us toll-free at (800) 929-2929 or email us at bkp.orders@aidcvt.com.

Host a Reading Group

For tips on how to form and carry on a book reading group in your workplace or community, see our website at www.bkconnection.com.

Join the BK Community

Thousands of readers of our books have become part of the "BK Community" by participating in events featuring our authors, reviewing draft manuscripts of forthcoming books, spreading the word about their favorite books, and supporting our publishing program in other ways. If you would like to join the BK Community, please contact us at bkcommunity@bkpub.com.